THE
EVERYTHING.

BRAZILIAN PORTUGUESE
PHRASE BOOK

Dear Reader,

Tudo bem? Thank you for picking up *The Everything®
Brazilian Portuguese Phrase Book,* my third book
with Adams Media. In it you will find the most helpful expressions and advice for successful communication in Brazilian Portuguese while traveling.

When I was preparing to write this book, I
thought about being a tourist myself. When I visit
a new country, even though I might not speak the
language fluently, it makes me feel good when I
make an effort to communicate in the language of
the locals. It's not just a question of pride; it's a deep
respect for the culture I am experiencing. I hope
this book will provide you with the tools to feel
that same way.

Try hard to use as much Portuguese as you can
while traveling—you'll find that Brazilians are generally very receptive to your efforts to speak their
language.

Fernanda Ferreira, PhD

The EVERYTHING Series

These handy, accessible books give you all you need to tackle a difficult project, gain a new hobby, or even brush up on something you learned back in school but have since forgotten. You can read from cover to cover or just pick out information from our four useful boxes.

 Alerts: Urgent warnings

 Essentials: Quick handy tips

 Facts: Important snippets of information

 Questions: Answers to common questions

When you're done reading, you can finally say you know **EVERYTHING®**!

PUBLISHER Karen Cooper
MANAGING EDITOR, EVERYTHING® SERIES Lisa Laing
COPY CHIEF Casey Ebert
ASSOCIATE PRODUCTION EDITOR Mary Beth Dolan
ACQUISITIONS EDITOR Kate Powers
ASSOCIATE DEVELOPMENT EDITOR Eileen Mullan
EVERYTHING® SERIES COVER DESIGNER Erin Alexander

THE
EVERYTHING®
Brazilian Portuguese Phrase Book

Learn basic Brazilian Portuguese
phrases—for any situation!

Fernanda Ferreira, PhD

Adamsmedia
Avon, Massachusetts

Published by
Adams Media, a division of F+W Media, Inc.
57 Littlefield Street, Avon, MA 02322. U.S.A.
www.adamsmedia.com

The Everything® Brazilian Portuguese Phrase Book contains mate-
rial adapted and abridged from *The Everything® Learning Brazilian
Portuguese Book* by Fernanda L. Ferreira, PhD, copyright © 2007 by
F+W Media, Inc., ISBN 10: 1-59869-277-1, ISBN 13: 978-1-59869-277-8.

ISBN 10: 1-4405-5527-3
ISBN 13: 978-1-4405-5527-5
eISBN 10: 1-4405-5528-1
eISBN 13: 978-1-4405-5528-2

Printed in the United States of America.

10 9 8 7 6 5 4 3 2 1

*This book is available at quantity discounts for bulk purchases.
For information, please call 1-800-289-0963.*

To Shannon, who always has the right phrase at the right time.

ACKNOWLEDGMENTS

Many thanks to Kate Powers and to all of the folks at Adams Media for their guidance along the way. Lisa Laing took on responsibilities when Kate left to pursue her academic dreams; thank you. Many of my friends—Jessie Bel, Anne Doyle, Viviane Gontijo, Lori Lecomte, Cristina Perissinotto, and Yulia Stakhnevich—helped me write this book by creating an intricate system of rewards that consisted of Friday night outings, Saturday brunches, Sunday trips to the beach, and occasional drives to ice cream stands. Shannon Fuller made sure that I followed the steps in order while writing the book. Elizabeth Wilson kept me sane, on a weekly basis. Last but not least, Floyd Ferreira took care of the house while I was away. Thank you.

Contents

CHAPTER 1

Introduction to Brazilian Portuguese

Portuguese is spoken by close to 200 million people, in far-reaching parts of the globe, such as Angola, Cape Verde, Guinea Bissau, Mozambique, and even Goa (India) and Macau (China). Brazil is by far the largest and most populated country where Portuguese is the official language. Thus, many people are interested in learning the Brazilian dialect. There are significant differences between the Brazilian and the European dialect, such as vocabulary, pronunciation, and word order. Nevertheless, with a lot of patience and repetition, speakers of each dialect can understand each other. If you picked up this book because you are traveling to Brazil, that was an excellent choice. If you decide to travel to Portugal, you can still use this book and apply some of the same useful phrases. We all share the same language.

Why Portuguese?

Have you ever listened to a *bossa nova* love song and wondered what the lyrics mean? Perhaps after years of careful contemplation, you finally booked that dream vacation to Brazil, and you want to learn how to speak like a native Brazilian. Maybe your grandparents emigrated from the Azores, Madeira, or Portugal, and you always wanted to write to them in their language. Or you might even be interested in learning Portuguese phrases to communicate with your coworkers or people you meet during a vacation.

Many people in the world speak Portuguese. You might be interested to know that many African and Asian countries have Portuguese as their official language. In addition, there is a growing Portuguese-speaking population in the United States. And because it is such an uncommonly taught language, learning a few phrases from this beautiful language will certainly impress your friends and family; it will help you understand the lyrics of famous *bossa nova* songs or the prose of an incredibly diverse body of literature.

Whatever the reason, be it personal enrichment, learning more about the diversity of Latin America, or discovering new worlds of cuisine, literature, and history, learning how to communicate in Brazilian Portuguese is a great step in your life. So put on your *samba* shoes and let's get started!

Portuguese: A Romance Language

Portuguese is a Romance language, which does not mean that it is full of loving words, but simply that it originated from Latin, the language of the Roman Empire. Along with other Romance languages, Portuguese came from Vulgar Latin, which simply meant that it was the "common," everyday speech of soldiers, farmers, settlers, and slaves of the Roman Empire.

Romance languages include Italian, French, Spanish, Galician, Romanian, and Catalan. There are also minority languages such as Occitan, Provençal, Friulian, and Ladin, among many other tongues whose origins can be traced back to Latin. With the decline of the Roman Empire in the fifth century, Vulgar Latin began to change slowly, taking on the diverse features and styles of the localities where it was spoken, thus generating the incredible array of Romance languages. The Visigoths, a group of barbaric tribes that invaded the Iberian Peninsula, added to the development of Portuguese and Spanish.

 Fact

Portuguese is becoming more and more popular in Asia. The number of Portuguese speakers has grown in particular in Macau, China, due to the region's increase in diplomatic and economic relations with Portugal and other Lusophone countries. Similarly, there have been reports of an increase in East Timor's Portuguese-speaking population in recent years.

In the seventh century, the Moors, an Arabic ethnic group of northern Africa, invaded the south of Spain and Portugal. The effect of the Arabic language is still found today in Portuguese and Spanish words, such as arroz (rice) and algodão (cotton). With colonization efforts by Spain, Portugal, and France starting in the early fifteenth century, Romance languages began to be spoken in many different parts of the world. Today, two-thirds of Romance language speakers live outside of Europe. In the case of Portuguese, approximately eighty percent of its speakers are concentrated in Brazil.

Similarities to Spanish

Portuguese and Spanish can be called "sister languages" due to their intrinsic similarities. After all, they both derive from spoken Latin. The following table shows the similarities in orthography between these languages.

COMPARING PORTUGUESE TO SPANISH: PART I		
PORTUGUESE	SPANISH	ENGLISH
classe	*clase*	class
casa	*casa*	house
livro	*libro*	book
caderno	*cuaderno*	notebook

When using your knowledge of Spanish to help with your Portuguese, be mindful that these are different languages, and similarity in orthography does not always mean similarity in pronunciation. Always learn how to pronounce the "sounds" of Portuguese instead of relying on your Spanish. What about differences in words and meanings? The following list shows how these languages can vary significantly:

COMPARING PORTUGUESE TO SPANISH: PART II		
PORTUGUESE	SPANISH	ENGLISH
cedo	*temprano*	early
desenvolvimento	*desarrollo*	development
envelope	*sobre*	envelope
irmã	*hermana*	sister

If that wasn't enough, there are some tricky words which are commonly referred to as "false cognates." These words sound similar to English or Spanish but mean something completely different in your target language, in this case, Portuguese. The novice student needs to watch out for these "false friends." Here are a few examples:

FALSE COGNATES	
PORTUGUESE	SPANISH
tirar (to take)	*tirar* (to throw away)
escritório (office)	*escritorio* (desk)
embaraçada (confused, ashamed)	*embarazada* (pregnant)

The trick here is to use a good Portuguese-English dictionary and always make sure you are saying the correct word, depending on the social situation. Some awkward moments may occur, but most of the time native speakers will understand and help you out.

European Portuguese Versus Brazilian Portuguese

When the Portuguese arrived in Brazil in the early sixteenth century, they found many speakers of different Native American languages already living there. It has been estimated that there were more than 1,000 indigenous languages spoken in Brazil at the time of the Portuguese arrival. With the advancement of white populations into the coastal areas of Brazil, these populations were slowly decimated by disease or genocide, so that nowadays we are left with about 170 different Native Brazilian languages in Brazil.

The development of Brazilian Portuguese is a complex one, but one that is fascinating nonetheless. Portuguese colonization in Brazil really started in 1548 with the introduction of a system of capitanias or territories awarded to Portuguese officials on a hereditary basis. Most of these territories failed economically, except for São Vicente (today's São Paulo state) and Pernambuco. Later, there was a system of governorships that responded directly to the King of Portugal. With the invasion of Portugal by Napoleon, the Portuguese Royal family transferred to Rio de Janeiro. This transatlantic move had a significant impact on the Portuguese educational policy in Brazil, especially with regard to the development of language instruction.

The path followed by Brazil since it became independent in 1822 was very different from that followed by other Portuguese colonies such as Angola and Mozambique. In these countries, the Portuguese-speaking community is a learned minority. In Brazil, Portuguese has been spoken by many generations of Brazilians, giving it a distinctly Brazilian flavor. Also, one has to account for linguistic contact with the Brazilian indigenous population, whose languages, including Tupi Guarani and others, also contributed words to the Brazilian dialect.

 Fact

In 2002, the city of São Gabriel da Cachoeira, a municipality in the state of Amazonas, passed a law making the indigenous languages Nheengatu, Tukano, and Boniwa official languages along with Portuguese.

In addition, one cannot forget the influence of millions of black Africans who were forcibly brought to Brazil to work in the sugarcane fields, gold mines, and the homes of Portuguese masters. These Bantu and Kwa language speakers offered a unique twist to the way Portuguese is spoken in Brazil.

WORDS OF INDIGENOUS ORIGIN IN BRAZILIAN PORTUGUESE

BRAZILIAN PORTUGUESE	ENGLISH
plants	
abacaxi	pineapple
caju	cashew fruit
animals	
piranha	piranha
sucuri	anaconda
arara	macaw
place names	
Guanabara	
Jacarepaguá	
Tijuca	
personal names	
Araci	
Iracema	
supernatural beings	
Tupã	supreme being of the Tupi people
Curupira	human-like creature whose feet are backwards; brings bad luck or death to those who see him

Reading and Pronouncing Portuguese

PRONUNCIATION GUIDE: THE PORTUGUESE LETTERS

LETTER	PORTUGUESE NAME	PRONUNCIATION	EXAMPLE	APPROXIMATE ENGLISH SOUND
a	a	AH	*casa*	**f**ather
b	bê	BEH	*berço*	**b**asement

LETTER	PORTUGUESE NAME	PRONUNCIATION	EXAMPLE	APPROXIMATE ENGLISH SOUND
c	cê	SEH	*centro*	**c**ent
			com	**c**omb
d	dê	DEH	*dado*	**d**ance
e	é or ê	EH	*ele*	b**ay**
f	efe	EH-fee	*fala*	**f**act
g	gê	JEH	*gente*	mea**s**ure
h	agá	a-GAH	*hospital*	[*silent*]
i	i	EE	*cinco*	s**ee**k
j	jota	JOH-tah	*já*	plea**s**ure
k	ká	KAH	*kiwi*	**k**itchen
l	ele	EH-lee	*lavar*	**l**oud
m	eme	EH-mee	*mesa*	**m**ouse
n	ene	EH-nee	*não*	**n**ever
o	ó or ô	AW or OH	*óbvio*	**awe**
p	pê	PEH	*pão*	**p**aint
q	quê	KEH	*quinze*	**k**ey
r	erre	EH-hee	*Rio*	**h**eap
			erro	un**h**ealthy
s	esse	EH-see	*santo*	**s**imple
t	tê	TEH	*tempo*	**s**t**eak**
u	u	OOH	*cajú*	j**u**ice
v	vê	VEH	*veja*	**v**ery
x	xis	SHEES	*roxo*	**sh**oe
w	dáblio	DAH-blee-oo	*watt*	**w**ater
y	ípsilon	EEP-see-laun	*Yara*	**y**ear
z	zê	ZEH	*zinco*	**z**ebra

There are also special letters and combinations of letters that make up unexpected sounds in Portuguese. These are:

SPECIAL LETTERS AND COMBINATIONS OF LETTERS			
LETTERS	PORTUGUESE EXAMPLE	ENGLISH TRANSLATION	PRONUNCIATION
–ç–	*caça*	hunt	pronounced like **s** KAH-sah
–nh–	*tamanho*	size	a little softer than the Spanish **ñ** tah-MANH-ny-oo
	façanha	feat	fah-SAHN-ny-ah
–lh–	*filho*	son	like the middle sound in "medallion" FEE-lyee-oo
	trabalho	work	trah-BAH-lyee-oo
–ch–	*chá*	tea	pronounced as in **sho**vel SHAH

Accent Marks

In Portuguese, accent marks help with the correct pronunciation of words. They indicate to the reader where to put emphasis in the word, or even if a vowel is more "open" or "closed." It is important to become familiar with these special diacritic marks.

ACCENT MARKS		
MARKS	NAME IN ENGLISH	NAME IN PORTUGUESE
á, é, í, ó, ú	acute	*acento agudo*
ê, ô	circumflex	*acento circunflexo*
à	grave	*acento grave*

MARKS	NAME IN ENGLISH	NAME IN PORTUGUESE
ã, õ	tilde	*til*
ü	dieresis	*trema*

 Essential

Accent marks and the sounds they create are not immediately intuitive to the second language learner. When learning Portuguese, give yourself time to figure out where to include these accents. As you read more and more materials in Portuguese, keep track of the accents and where they usually go in the word. Familiarity with the written word will boost your confidence and spelling accuracy in Portuguese!

The Letter C

Before vowels *e* or *i*, this letter has a soft *s* sound as in the English word "for**c**e." Examples are *centro* "center" and *cinco* "five." However, before vowels *a, o, u*, and most consonants, the letter has a hard *k* sound as in the English word "**c**oat." Some examples are *casa* "house," *comida* "food," *cuidado* "care," *crédito* "credit," or *clínica* "clinic."

The Letter G

This letter often creates a sound that does not appear at the beginning of English words, but can be found in the middle of the word "mea**s**ure." In Portuguese, it appears at the beginning of words when the vowels *e* or *i* follow it, such as in *gente* "people" and *ginásio* "gym." It has a hard sound when it appears before vowels *a, o,* *u*, and other consonants, as in the English word "**g**ame." Examples are *gato* "cat," *gota* "drop," *guri* "young boy," and *grande* "big."

The Letter *S*

This letter can be used to create two different but closely related sounds. The first is very similar to the sound in English words "**s**ink" and "ca**s**t." The Portuguese examples are *sopa* "soup," *esse* "this one," and *lápis* "pencil." The second is a raspier *z* sound as in the English words "tho**s**e," "wi**s**dom," and "tran**s**it." The counterpart examples in Portuguese are *casada* "married," *desde* "since," and *trânsito* "traffic."

 **Question**

How can I practice my pronunciation?
Pronunciation isn't something that can be learned from a book. Hire a native speaker as a tutor, watch Brazilian movies, and listen to Brazilian music to develop an ear for spoken Portuguese.

The Letter *Z*

This letter is very similar to the English letter, especially in regard to the beginnings of words. As with the English word "**z**ebra," the same sound is found in Portuguese with *zero* "zero" and *prazer* "pleasure." However, this letter also has a sound similar to the English word "cook**s**" at the end of segments, such as in the Portuguese example *cartaz* "poster."

The Letter *T*

In some dialects of Brazilian Portuguese, such as the *carioca* (the name of the dialect from Rio de Janeiro), this letter can have a very unexpected sound. Before the vowels *i* and sometimes *e* (if unstressed and at the end of a word), it will produce a sound as in the English word "**ch**eer." Portuguese words such as *tipo* "type" and *elefante* "elephant" will sound like TCHEE-poh and eh-leh-FAHN-tchee. This does not happen in all contexts. In dialects spoken elsewhere in Brazil, the letter *t* will sounds like a soft English *t*, without the aspiration. So *inteligente* would sound like een-teh-lee-GEHN-tee. In the case of the letter appearing before other vowels and consonants, it will sound like the English word "**t**ime" (without the added aspiration). Portuguese examples are *terra* "earth" and *trem* "train."

All *-te* endings in Brazilian Portuguese can have a hard "tee" sound or a raspier "tchee" one, depending on the dialectal region where you are from. Rio de Janeiro speakers prefer the latter.

The Letter *D*

When the letter *d* comes in close contact with the letter *i*, an unexpected sound is produced. Much like the sound in the English word "**j**eans," the Portuguese word *dia* "day" might be pronounced like JEE-ah. Before all other phonological contexts, the letter stands for the sound as in the English word "**d**en," yielding Portuguese examples such as *dar* "give" and *droga* "drug."

The Letter *R*

This letter has two basic sounds, which are very different from the English *r*. First, it is pronounced like the *h* in the English word "**h**eat." Some Portuguese examples include *rua* "street," *dor* "pain," *guardanapo* "napkin," *carro* "car," and *genro* "son-in-law." Second, this letter in Portuguese is pronounced similarly to the *t* in the middle of English words "le**tt**er" or "la**t**er." It can be found in Portuguese words such as *caro* "expensive" and *branco* "white."

 Essential

Since the sound that is made when the letter *i* comes after *t* or *d* is primarily used by those who speak in a Rio de Janeiro dialect, a more economically developed area of Brazil, it is seen as a more prestigious pronunciation. However, in the north, northeast, and south of Brazil, this pronunciation is mostly ignored and speakers communicate successfully pronouncing the *t* and the *d* similarly to the English letters.

The Letter *L*

The one thing to remember about this letter is that at the end of words, the *l* sounds like a *w* as in the English word "no**w**." So the Portuguese word *Brasil* sounds like BRAH-zeew. The letter behaves like the English letter *l* at the beginning of words.

 **Essential**

> You will notice that Brazilians will leave out the *r* sound at the end of words, such as *amor* "love" or *chamar* "to call." This is not seen as a reflection of uneducated speech or laziness, but rather an evolution of the language. The same happened with French, whose final consonants are almost never pronounced! In order to sound more native, make sure to drop those end-word *r*'s in Portuguese!

The Letters *M* and *N*

As you might have noticed, Portuguese has many nasal sounds. The letters *m* and *n*, when appearing at the end of a word or syllable, are an indication that the previous vowel is nasalized. Thus, the combination of vowel plus *m* or *n* should not be perceived as two different sounds (vowel plus consonant), but actually a nasal-sounding vowel. Portuguese words such as *sim* "yes" and *bom* "good" are pronounced by forcing more air out of your nostrils and avoiding putting your lips together at the end. The letters behave like the English letters when they come at the beginning of a word such as *mesa* "table" and *navio* "boat."

The Letter *X*

Amazingly, there are four different sounds that can be created when this letter appears in Portuguese words. The first is similar to the English word "**sh**eep." Portuguese examples include *xadrez* "chess" and *lixo* "trash." The second sound is similar to the English word "fi**x**," as in the Portuguese *complexo* "complex." Thirdly, this letter can sound like a normal *s*, as with the English word "fea**st**." Portuguese examples are *excluir* "to exclude" and *excepcional* "exceptional." Finally, it is very common to hear a *z* sound as in the English word "amazing." Portuguese examples are *exótico* "exotic" and *roxo* "purple."

WORD STRESS

NEXT-TO-LAST SYLLABLE	LAST SYLLABLE	THIRD-TO-LAST SYLLABLE
piloto pilot	*café* coffee	*capítulo* chapter
imagem image	*baú* chest	*código* code
contente happy	*açaí* a tropical fruit	*árvore* tree
fácil easy	*dominó* domino	*fósforo* match
all verbs in infinitives ending in -*r*, *amar* to love		
all nasal diphthongs ending the word, *irmão* brother		

THE VOWEL A

TYPE	ENGLISH WORD	CONTEXT	PORTUGUESE EXAMPLES
Stressed	f**a**ther, c**o**t	AH	*garfo* GAHR-foo "fork," *caro* KAH-roo "expensive"
Unstressed	tub**a**	ah	*porta* POHR-t**a**h "door," *filha* FEE-ly-**a**h "daughter"
Nasal		before nasal consonants or with tilde	*ba**n**ho* BANH-ny-oo "bath," *irm**ã*** eehr-MAHN "sister"

THE VOWEL E

TYPE	ENGLISH WORD	CONTEXT	PORTUGUESE EXAMPLES
Open	n**et**	written with the acute é	*café* kah-FEH "coffee"
Closed	--	written with a circumflex ê	*pêssego* PEH-she-goo "peach"
Longer	m**e**	at the end of a word	*filme* FEEL-mee "movie"
		at the end of a one-syllable word	*de* "of," *e* "and"
Nasal	--	before nasal consonants	*senha* SEHN-ny-ah "passcode" *bem* BEHN-ee "well"

THE VOWEL I

TYPE	ENGLISH WORD	CONTEXT	PORTUGUESE EXAMPLES
Longer	s**ee**	at the end of a syllable	*saí,* "(I) left," *país,* "country," *raiz,* "root"
Shorter	sa**y**	at the end of a the word	*pai,* "father," *leite,* "milk"
Nasal	--	before nasal consonants	*tinha,* "(he) had," *sim,* "yes"

THE VOWEL O

TYPE	ENGLISH WORD	CONTEXT	PORTUGUESE EXAMPLES
Open	s**aw**	written with the acute ó	*dominó,* "domino"
Closed	--	written with a circumflex ô	*complô,* "scheme"

THE VOWEL O (CONTINUED)

TYPE	ENGLISH WORD	CONTEXT	PORTUGUESE EXAMPLES
Longer	gl**ue**	at the end of a word	*pato* "duck"
		at the end of a one-syllable word	*do* "of the," *o* "the"
Nasal	--	before nasal consonants	*sonho* "dream," *com* "with"

THE VOWEL U

TYPE	ENGLISH WORD	CONTEXT	PORTUGUESE EXAMPLES
Longer	t**oo**th	at the end of a syllable/word	*cajú* "cashew fruit," *tu* "you," *grúa* "crane"
Shorter	bo**w**	at the end of the word	*pau* "wood" or "stick," *nau* "boat"
		in the combinations *qua* and *gua*	*quadro* "board," *guarda* "policeman"
Nasal	--	before nasal consonants	*punha* "(he) would put," *um* "one"

 Alert

The vowel *u* is silent when used in the combinations *que, qui, gue,* and *gui.* In these cases, only pronounce the "hard" consonants, as in *queijo* "cheese," *quinze* "fifteen," *guerra* "war," and *guitarra* "electric guitar."

Aside from oral and nasal vowels, there are vowel combinations in Portuguese. When they are in the same syllable, they are called diphthongs.

ORAL DIPHTHONGS	
APPROXIMATE ENGLISH SOUND	PORTUGUESE EXAMPLES
my	*pai* PAH-ee "father"
cow	*autor* ah-oo-TOH "author"
--	*papéis* pah-PEH-yees "papers"
hay	*rei* HEY "king"
--	*deus* DEH-oohs "god"
--	*céu* SEH-oo "sky"
--	*oi* OH-ee "hi"
coy	*dói* DOH-ee "(it) hurts"
--	*viu* VEE-oo "(she) saw"
--	*cuidado* koo-yee-DAH-doo "careful"

NASAL DIPHTHONGS	
APPROXIMATE ENGLISH SOUND	PORTUGUESE
AHN-ee	*mãe* "mother"
AHN-oo	*cão* "dog"
OHN-ee	*põe* "(she) puts"

Hiatus

A hiatus is a combination of vowels in separate syllables. While diphthongs are two graphic vowels put together (one pronounced longer and slower than the other), the hiatus expresses two strong vowels very clearly. Here are some examples:

- *tia* "aunt," *rua* "street"
- *caos* "chaos"
- *rio* "river"

 Alert

There are some nasal diphthongs that are not expressed orthographically with the ~ (tilde), but rather with nasal consonants. This is the case with words ending in *em* or *en*, as in *porém* "but" and *podem* "(they) can." In addition, there is one special nasal diphthong that starts with a nasal consonant: *muito* "many" or "very."

Typing in Portuguese

When writing electronically, it is important to add the accent symbols and diacritics that are part of the Portuguese language. There is a big difference between an accented vowel *é* (is) and one without an accent *e* (and). The following table shows how to add these accents into your electronic documents.

WINDOWS KEYS	RESULT
Control + ' [apostrophe], then any vowel	á, é, í, ó, ú
Control + ` [grave], then a	à
Control + Shift + ~ [tilde], then vowel	ã, õ
Control + , [comma], then c	ç

APPLE KEYS	RESULT
Option + e, then any vowel	á, é, í, ó, ú
Option + ` [grave], then a	à

APPLE KEYS	RESULT
Option + n, then vowel	ã, õ
Option + c	ç

Introduction to Nouns

Nouns refer to persons, places, and things. While learning a second language, make lists of nouns that you want to learn. It is easier to learn nouns because they often refer to something concrete. However, they also refer to abstract elements, ideas, and qualities. In Portuguese, nouns fall under two categories: masculine or feminine. The words *mesa* "table," *bolsa* "bag," and *chave* "key" belong to the feminine gender; while *caderno* "notebook," *livro* "book," and *pente* "comb" are masculine. Most of the time you can tell by the ending of the word which gender it belongs to. However, there are some tricky examples, such as the ones that end in *-e* (*chave* and *pente*), which can be either feminine or masculine. See the gender classification table below.

PORTUGUESE NOUNS	
MASCULINE	**FEMININE**
livro book	*mochila* backpack
tio uncle	*tia* aunt
espelho mirror	*escola* school
quadro blackboard	*mesa* table
título title	*página* page
gesto gesture	*janela* window

Keep in mind that nouns that end in -*o* are overwhelmingly masculine. Second, nouns that end in (unstressed) -*a* are normally feminine. What if a noun does not end in either of those vowels? Here are some general rules.

NOUNS ENDING IN CONSONANTS -L, -R, AND –Z, THE VOWEL -U, AND THE LETTERS –UME ARE MASCULINE	
PORTUGUESE	**ENGLISH**
hotel	hotel
casal	married couple
mar	sea
professor	teacher, professor
rapaz	young man
cartaz	poster
peru	turkey
tatu	armadillo
ciúme	jealousy
legume	vegetable

There are also nouns with different endings that are mostly feminine. Aside from the most common unstressed -*a* ending for feminine nouns, they can also be identified by other typical suffixes. The following table outlines those endings with some examples.

NOUNS ENDINGS IN LETTERS -DADE, -AGEM, AND -ÇÃO ARE NORMALLY FEMININE	
PORTUGUESE	ENGLISH
identidade	identity, ID card
liberdade	liberty
garagem	garage
viagem	trip
comunicação	communication
atenção	attention

 Alert

Most nouns that end in a stressed *-á* are masculine. For example, *chá* "tea" and *sofá* "sofa" as well as the names of countries such as *Canadá* and *Panamá*. Other nouns that end in a (without the accent, not stressed) are also masculine, in this case because of their Greek origin. One example is *o poema* oo-poh-EH-mah "the poem." The best way to learn the gender of these words is to write them down with the article, as in *o chá* "the tea." As you learn more words, continue adding them to your list.

MASCULINE GREEK ORIGIN WORDS ENDING IN –A	
PORTUGUESE	ENGLISH
o cinema	movie theater
o mapa	map
o planeta	planet
o problema	problem
o programa	program
o telefonema	phone call

 **Essential**

One tip to help you learn the gender of nouns is to write them together in categories. With any list of vocabulary that you learn, you should find ways in which words can be connected (be it "school objects," "home appliances," or "my favorite clothes"). Think of your brain as a closet that is organized in drawers. If you put socks and shirts in their own designated places, it will be easier to retrieve them later. The same happens with Portuguese words!

Definite and Indefinite Articles

Before each noun, it is common for speakers to say an article, such as "the" or "a/an." In Portuguese, these small but essential words follow gender classification. Definite articles are so called because they refer to specific or "definite" things and places. On the other hand, "indefinite" articles refer to elements that are not previously specified or are general in nature.

DEFINITE ARTICLES		
	MASCULINE	**FEMININE**
Singular	*o livro* "**the** book"	*a mesa* "**the** table"
Plural	*os livros* "**the** books"	*as mesas* "**the** tables"

There are four ways of saying "the" in Portuguese, depending on the gender and the number of the noun. Portuguese uses the definite article more often than in

English. For example, when referring to "friends and family," Portuguese speakers say *os amigos* "(the) friends" and *a família* "(the) family." Common expressions in English such as "love is blind" would be translated in Portuguese as *o amor é cego*. Definite articles are even common when referring to proper names! It is common to hear people address others in some parts of Brazil by adding a definite article such as in *o Paulo* "Paul" or literally "the Paul." Finally, one of the most interesting features of Portuguese is the fact that Portuguese speakers might opt to say *o meu livro*, literally "(the) my book" when using possessive pronouns.

INDEFINITE ARTICLES		
	MASCULINE	**FEMININE**
Singular	*um livro* "**a** book"	*uma mesa* "**a** table"
Plural	*uns livros* "**some** books"	*umas mesas* "**some** tables"

The important thing to remember is that indefinite articles are used for non-specific things, so you might say *eu li um livro* "I read a book," or you might say *eu li o livro de Português* for "I read the Portuguese book," which is more specific.

Demonstratives

When traveling, it is common to point and refer to things and people by including a demonstrative, such as "this" or "that" before it, depending on the relative distance involved.

In Portuguese, speakers follow a familiar system of gender and number agreement.

NUMBER	MASCULINE	FEMININE	ENGLISH
singular	*este/esse*	*esta/essa*	this
plural	*estes/esses*	*estas/essas*	these
singular	*aquele*	*aquela*	that
plural	*aqueles*	*aquelas*	those

DEMONSTRATIVES IN PORTUGUESE

 **Essential**

There are also neutral forms that are used when the referent is unknown or not determined by gender. So, use the words **isto** and **isso** "this" and **aquilo** "that" by themselves when referring to unknown concepts. These are very handy words to have in your repertoire, especially when you want to know what things are in Portuguese.

Common Contractions

When using prepositions ("to," "from") followed by determiners (the articles and demonstratives), these words come together and "contract" or combine in order to form a different, shorter word. Here are some "common contractions" in Portuguese.

USING "FROM + THE" IN PORTUGUESE		
PREPOSITION + DEFINITE ARTICLE	**CONTRACTION**	**ENGLISH**
de + o	*do*	from the (masculine singular)
de + a	*da*	from the (feminine singular)
de + os	*dos*	from the (masc./mixed gender plural)
de + as	*das*	from the (fem. plural)

When would you have to use these contractions? For example, when saying sentences that refer to your origin, such as *Eu sou **dos** Estados Unidos* "I am **from the** United States." Thus, when saying *Ele é **do** Brazil*, you are literally saying "He is **from the** Brazil." Here are some examples of common contractions:

*Eu sou **do** Brasil, e você?*
(I am **from** Brazil, how about you?)

*Eu sou **dos** Estados Unidos. E a Ana?*
(I am **from the** United States. And Anna?)

*Ela é **da** França.*
(She's **from** France.)

É mesmo? E o Jacques? De onde ele é?
(Really? And Jacques? Where's he from?)

*Eu acho que ele é **do** Canadá.*
(I think he's **from** Canada.)

*Não, eu sou **das** Filipinas!*
(No, I'm **from the** Philippines!)

Notice that countries have a gender and a number, and thus must follow the same gender/number system spelled out in previous sections. You would have to know the "gender" and "number" of the country, and if a definite article is used, in order to say these sentences correctly.

 Alert

> Some countries do not require the use of the definite article (*o, a, os, as*) when they are mentioned, so there is no contraction, just the bare preposition. The most noted examples are *Ela é **de** Portugal* "She's from Portugal," *Ele é **de** Mozambique* "He's from Mozambique," and *Eles são **de** Cuba* "They are from Cuba."

Another common contraction is between the preposition *em* "in, on, at" and the definite articles. Here are the examples:

USING "IN THE" IN PORTUGUESE		
PREPOSITION + DEFINITE ARTICLE	**CONTRACTION**	**ENGLISH**
em + o	*no*	in the (masc. sing.)
em + a	*na*	in the (fem. sing.)
em + os	*nos*	in the (masc./mixed gender plural)
em + as	*nas*	in the (fem. plural)

When would you use these contractions? How about when talking about where you live? Here is a sample dialogue that includes some of these contractions:

Cláudio, onde você mora?
(Cláudio, where do you live?)

*Eu moro **no** estado do Ceará, **no** Brasil.*
(I live **in the** state of Ceará, **in** Brazil.)

Nossa, e você, Nilda?
(Wow, and you, Nilda?)

*Eu moro **na** ilha de São Vicente, Cabo Verde.*
(I live **in the** island of São Vicente, Cabo Verde.)

Eu adoraria visitar vocês dois.
(I would love to visit both of you.)

*Você será sempre bem-vinda **na** nossa casa!*
(You are always welcome **in** our house!)

Do indefinite articles contract? Sure! The following shows the common contractions involving the preposition *em* "in, on" and the indefinite articles *um, uma* "a/an."

USING "IN + A/SOME" IN PORTUGUESE		
PREPOSITION + INEFINITE ARTICLE	**CONTRACTION**	**ENGLISH**
em + um	*num*	in a (masc. sing.)
em + uma	*numa*	in a (fem. sing.)
em + uns	*nuns*	in some (plural)

To express indefinite ideas, a speaker could use these indefinite pronouns. For example, one could say *Eu vivo **num** bairro elegante* "I live **in an** elegant neighborhood," or

*Eu estudo **numa** universidade muito cara* "I study **in a** very expensive university." Notice that in these two examples, the places were not specifically mentioned.

Cognates

Because both Portuguese and English are Indo-European languages, some words in Portuguese have a similar spelling to English, and are thus easy to identify and guess their meaning. Here is a short list:

* *acidente*
* *ator*
* *adorável*
* *animal*
* *automóvel*
* *bagagem*
* *catedral*
* *central*
* *ciclista*
* *condutor*
* *conversível*
* *criatura*
* *crime*
* *cruel*

* *elefante*
* *famoso*
* *favor*
* *físico*
* *futebol*
* *hospital*
* *hotel*
* *humor*
* *idéia*
* *importante*
* *inevitável*
* *informação*
* *inventar*
* *local*

* *motor*
* *música*
* *natural*
* *plano*
* *popular*
* *potente*
* *presidente*
* *rádio*
* *respeitável*
* *sinistro*
* *táxi*
* *telefone*

In order to identify how to say some words in Portuguese that could have English spelling equivalents, here is a list of similar endings:

SPELLING EQUIVALENTS	
PORTUGUESE WORD	**ENGLISH EQUIVALENT**
psicologia	psychology
see-koh-loh-JEE-yah	
autonomia	autonomy
ah-oo--toh-noh-MEE-yah	

Nouns that end in *-ica* in Portuguese usually end in "-ic(s)" in English.

SPELLING EQUIVALENTS	
PORTUGUESE WORD	**ENGLISH EQUIVALENT**
física	physics
FEE-zee-kah	
música	music
MOO-zee-kah	

Nouns that end in *-ade* in Portuguese usually end in "-ty" in English.

SPELLING EQUIVALENTS	
PORTUGUESE WORD	**ENGLISH EQUIVALENT**
universidade	university
oo-nee-vehr-see-DAH-dee	
autoridade	authority
ah-oo--toh-ree-DAH-dee	

Nouns that end in *-ista* in Portuguese usually end in "-ist" in English.

SPELLING EQUIVALENTS	
PORTUGUESE WORD	**ENGLISH EQUIVALENT**
dentista dehn-TEES-tah	dentist
artista ahr-TEES-tah	artist

Nouns that end in *-ário* in Portuguese usually end in "-ary" in English.

SPELLING EQUIVALENTS	
PORTUGUESE WORD	**ENGLISH EQUIVALENT**
comentário koh-mehn-TAH-ree-oo	commentary
dicionário dee-see-oh-NAH-ree-oo	dictionary

Some nouns that end in *-or* in Portuguese also end in "-or" in English.

SPELLING EQUIVALENTS	
PORTUGUESE WORD	**ENGLISH EQUIVALENT**
professor proh-feh-SOHR	professor
ator ah-TOHR	actor

Nouns that end in *-ção* in Portuguese usually end in "-ion" in English.

SPELLING EQUIVALENTS	
PORTUGUESE WORD	**ENGLISH EQUIVALENT**
estação ehs-tah-SAHN-oo	station
religião heh-lee-gee-AHN-oo	religion

Nouns that end in *-cia* in Portuguese usually end in "-ce" in English.

SPELLING EQUIVALENTS	
PORTUGUESE WORD	**ENGLISH EQUIVALENT**
importância een-pohr-TAHN-see-ah	importance
independência een-deh-pehn-DEHN-see-ah	independence

Some adjectives ending in *-al* in Portuguese also end in "-al" in English.

SPELLING EQUIVALENTS	
PORTUGUESE WORD	**ENGLISH EQUIVALENT**
especial ees-peh-see-AHL	special
local loh-KAHL	local

Adjectives ending in *-oso* usually end in "-ous" in English.

SPELLING EQUIVALENTS

PORTUGUESE WORD	ENGLISH EQUIVALENT
religioso heh-lee-gee-OH-zoo	religious
amoroso ah-moh-ROH-zoo	amorous

False Friends

A "false friend" (or a false cognate) is a word that looks like the same word in your own language, but has a different meaning in the language you are learning. The following section will help you to avoid many common mistakes. There are numerous false friends in Portuguese and English!

 Fact

> There are thousands of cognates between Portuguese and English, but some of them can be false friends! Make sure you know the true meaning of a word before working it into your spoken language.

FALSE COGNATES

assistir ah-sees-TEEHR	to attend or to watch, not to assist
delito deh-LEE-too	crime, not delight
recordar heh-kohr-DAH	to remember, not to record

CHAPTER 2

Introducing Yourself

You will find that this book has many ready-made sentences and expressions to help you communicate in a variety of situations. However, it is still very important to know the basics of the language. Once you understand how sentences and phrases are formed, they will make a lot more sense to you.

The Verbs *Ser*, *Estar*, and *Ter*

Let's start with three very basic verbs. They are not only very common; they also have very irregular conjugations. Refer to the following examples.

SER: To Be

The verb *ser* (to be) is one of the most commonly used verbs in Portuguese. It is important to learn this verb inside and out, as you will hear it in almost every conversation you have!

In the present tense, it is conjugated as follows:

SINGULAR		PLURAL	
eu sou	I am	*nós somos*	we are
EH-oo SO		Noyes SON-moos	
você é	you are	*Vocês são*	you (all) are
voh-SAY EH		voh-SAY-ees SAHN-oo	
ele é	he is	*eles são*	they are
EH-lee EH		EH-lees SAHN-oo	
ela é	she is	*eles são*	they are
EH-lah EH		EH-lees SAHN-oo	

 Fact

It is common, but not required, to omit the subject pronoun in both spoken and written Portuguese. In fact, you will sound more "native" if you do not say the subject pronoun and only use the conjugated verb.

I am American.
Eu sou americano.
eh-oo SOH ah-meh-ree-KAHN-noo

I am American.
Sou americano.
SOH ah-meh-ree-KAH-noo

I'm Paul, and you?
Sou Paul, e você?
soo "Paul" ee voh-SAY

Ser is used when you want to indicate where you are from. It's normally followed by the preposition *de* + a place name (adding the possible contraction) when it serves that purpose.

We are from Boston.
Somos de Boston.
SOH-moos dee BOHS-tohn

To find out where someone is from, ask the question:
De onde você é?
dee ON-dee voh-SAY EH
De onde o senhor/a senhora é? (formal)
dee OHN-dee oo senh-ny-ohr / ah senh-ny-oh-rah EH?

Ser can be used to indicate possession when followed by the preposition *de* + a noun or a proper name:

It's my wife's suitcase.
É a maleta da minha esposa.
EH ah mah-LEH-tah dah MEE-ny-ah ehs-POH-zah.

It's John's.
É do John.
EH doo "John"

To find out to whom something belongs, ask the question:

Whose is it?
De quem é?
dee keyn EH

Whose are they?
De quem são?
dee keyn SAHN-oo

ESTAR: To Be

Meaning "to be," this verb is used quite a bit in Portuguese to express physical and emotional states. It is also used alongside other verbs to make up common structures, such as the progressive tense. Here's the conjugation in the present indicative.

THE VERB *ESTAR* IN THE PRESENT TENSE

eu **estou**	ehs-TOH-oo	I am
você **está**	ehs-TAH	you are
ele/ela **está**	ehs-TAH	he/she/it is
nós **estamos**	ehs-TAH-moos	we are
vocês **estão**	ehs-TAHN-oo	you (all) are
eles/elas **estão**	ehs-TAHN-oo	they are

 Alert

It is important to pronounce the forms **estou** (*eu* form) and **estão** (*vocês/eles* form) very clearly since they might sound similar at the beginning. When Brazilians are talking, they will very often cut off the first syllable **es-** of these verb forms. Be prepared to hear **tou**, **tá**, **tamo(s)**, and **tão** in spoken conversation. You might even start saying them, too!

 Essential

Use a form of the verb *estar* with the adjectives and adverbs in the following table to express how people feel, look, or seem. Don't forget that some adjectives and adverbs need to "match" with their respective subjects, especially if the masculine form ends in -o. For example: *ele está cansado* "he is/looks tired;" *ela está cansada* "she is/seems tired." As you can see, sometimes the verb *estar* "to be" is used for the verbs "to seem," "to appear," or "to feel" in English because they reflect a condition or state, not an immutable physical characteristic. The following are some common physical states that are used with the verb *estar*.

SAMPLE SENTENCES WITH *ESTAR*

eu estou contente	I am happy
eh-oo ehs-TOH-oo kohn-TEHN-tee	
nós estamos cansados	we are tired
noh-ees ehs-TAH-moos kahn-SAH-doos	
elas estão bonitas hoje	they are pretty today
EH-lahs ehs-TAHN-oo boh-NEE-tahs OH-gee	

TER: To Have

In order to express things that you own, you must use the verb *ter*. Here's the conjugation in the present tense:

THE VERB *TER* IN THE PRESENT TENSE

eu tenho	I have
você tem	you have
ele/ela tem	he/she has
nós temos	we have
vocês têm	you (all) have
eles/elas têm	they have

Here are some sample sentences with this very useful verb:

SAMPLE SENTENCES WITH *TER*

O hotel tem muitos hóspedes.	The hotel has a lot of guests.
Eu tenho uma reserva para hoje.	I have a reservation for today.
Meus amigos têm meu endereço.	My friends have my address.
A cliente tem uma pergunta.	The client has a question.

You can also use the verb *ter* in an impersonal sense. This means that there is no clear subject, and the sentence is normally translated as "there is/are." See the following examples for the "existential" use of *ter*.

SAMPLE SENTENCES WITH EXISTENTIAL *TER*	
Tem muita gente no mercado.	There are a lot of people at the market.
Tem um mapa no balcão.	There is a map on the counter.
Tem uma padaria aqui perto.	There is a bakery near here.

Lastly, the verb *ter* can be used to mean "obligation." In this case, it is very similar to the structure in English "have to."

[SUBJECT]	*TER* [CONJUGATED]	QUE	VERB [INFINITIVE]
Eu	*tenho*	*que*	***acordar*** *às 8h.*
			I have to wake up at 8 A.M.
Você	*tem*	*que*	***fazer*** *a reserva.*
			You have to make the reservation.
Nós	*temos*	*que*	***seguir*** *este caminho.*
			We have to follow that path.

OBLIGATION: *TER QUE* + VERB

Notice that the first verb, *ter*, is written according to the subject. The second verb, in bold, is not conjugated: it's in the infinitive.

From Nouns to Pronouns

In order to make discourse less repetitive, speakers often substitute nouns for pronouns. For instance, instead of saying the phrase "my sister" again and again, you can say "she" when you are telling a story. That's a subject pronoun. There are also direct and indirect object pronouns, which also take the place of a noun that has already been mentioned. Here are some of these words that are essential in Portuguese:

PERSONAL PRONOUNS IN PORTUGUESE			
SINGULAR		**PLURAL**	
eu	I	*nós/a gente*	we
tu/você	you	*vocês*	you (all), y'all, you guys
ele	he	*eles*	they
ela	she	*elas*	they

There are two ways of referring to "we" in Brazilian Portuguese: *nós*, which is a little less used and more formal, and *a gente*, which is more colloquial. The important rule to follow when using these two personal pronouns is to conjugate the verb in the plural when using *nós* and in the singular when using *a gente*. *A gente* literally means "we the people," so it is grammatically singular, even though it refers to more than one person.

There are two forms of "you" in Portuguese. Listen to how the Brazilians are speaking and follow along. Some of this variation is based on the geographical region. In southern Brazil, the *tu* form is used regularly with its separate verb conjugation. In the big urban and cultural centers such as Rio de Janeiro and São Paulo, and the state of Minas Gerais, you might hear the form *você* as well as its reduced form *cê*. Finally, in many places in northeastern Brazil, such as in the cities of Recife and Fortaleza, the familiar *tu* is used, albeit with similar verb conjugations belonging to the *você* form. Although this might be daunting at first, if you stick to using *você* for "you," you cannot go wrong. No matter what region of Brazil you are visiting, you will be understood.

Alert

You might notice that more traditional Portuguese grammar includes the plural form *vós* for "you" or "y'all." This form is archaic and never used in Brazilian Portuguese. The possessive forms, *vosso* and *vossa* "yours," are uttered by many speakers from Portugal, but not in Brazil.

What about the levels of formality? When first introduced to an older gentleman or woman, use *o senhor* and *a senhora* respectively. Wait until they tell you that they do not mind being addressed by the *você* form.

When referring to people in the third or second person, it might be common to hear **Seu** *José* for "Mr. José" and **Dona** *Maria* for "Mrs. Maria" as a form of respect.

Here is a sample dialogue:

Robert: *Olá, Seu José, como vai?*
(Hello, Mr. José, how are you?)

José: *Bem, obrigado, Robert, e você?*
(Fine, thanks, Robert, and you?)

Robert: *Tudo bem, e como vai sua esposa, Dona Maria?* (Great, and how is your wife, Mrs. Maria?)

José: *Ela vai muito bem, obrigado.*
(She's very well, thanks.)

Direct Object Pronouns

A direct object is not the subject of a sentence. For example, in the sentence "I called **Maria**," Maria is not the subject. Maria is the recipient of the action or, in other words, the direct object of the verb. If you say "I called **her**," then you have used the "direct object pronoun," which means that this is the word that substitutes for the proper noun "Maria." Why do we use these pronouns? Read the conversation below:

Did you call Maria?

No, I did not call Maria.

Why didn't you call Maria?

Because I didn't want to talk to Maria.

The repetition of the direct object "Maria" sounds rather strange, doesn't it? In fact, speakers in many languages avoid this unnecessary repetition by using a pronoun "she" in place of the direct object. Here's a list of the direct object pronouns.

DIRECT OBJECT PRONOUNS	
me	me
te	you (sing., familiar)
o	him, it (masc. sing.)
a	her, it (fem. sing.)
nos	us
os	them (masc./mixed gender pural)
as	them (fem. plural)

The pronoun *vos* (you, plural) is not included because it is not used in Brazilian Portuguese except in certain formal contexts. It is, however, used extensively in Portugal. In order to express the plural "you" in Brazilian Portuguese, one must use *vocês* "you all," "y'all," "you guys." See the following examples:

*Ele **me** chamou.*	He called **me**.
EH-lee mee shah-MOH-oo	
*Eu **te** amo.*	I love **you**.
EH-oo tee AHN-moo	
*Nós amamos **vocês**!*	We love **you all**!
NOH-ees ah-MAHN-moos voh-SAYS	
*Eu **os** conheço.*	I know **them**.
EH-oo oos kohn-NYEH-soo	

Pay attention to the placement of the pronoun in relation to the conjugated verb. The direct object pronoun can go before, after, or even in the middle of the verb! However, speakers often do not follow the strict rules of grammar. In colloquial speech, Brazilian Portuguese speakers often use these pronouns before the verb when they should use them after the verb. Also, they might use the subject pronoun when they should use the object form instead. Here are some examples:

*Ela **me** viu.*	She saw **me**. (Brazilian
EH-lah mee VEE-oo	Portuguese)
*Ela viu-**me**.*	She saw **me**. (European
EH-lah VEE-oo mee	Portuguese)
*Eu **a** vi.*	I saw **her**. (Brazilian Portuguese,
EH-oo ah vee	prescriptive usage)
*Eu vi **ela**.*	I saw **her**. (Brazilian Portuguese,
EH-oo vee EH-lah	colloquial speech, subject form)

Learners should be aware that in everyday speech and even in popular media, the non-prescriptive use of the direct object is common.

In a negative sentence, the word *não* must come before the object pronoun.

He doesn't eat **it**.
*Ele não **o** come.*
EH-lee NAHN-oo KOHN-mee

Why don't you invite **them**?
*Porque você não **os** convida?* (formal, educated)
pohr-KEH voh-SAY nahn-oos kohn-VEE-dah?

*Porque você não convida **eles**?* (less standard,
colloquial)
pohr-keh voh-SAY nahn kohn-VEE-dah EH-lees?

 **Essential**

As far as saying goodbye, the same kissing rules apply:
one or two kisses for women, warm handshakes for
men. Don't be surprised if a Brazilian will kiss you three
times and say *três pra casar*, meaning "three times so
you can get married." This is sort of a little play with
the two-kiss rule, and one which can lead to closer
friendships.

Variation on Direct Object Pronoun Forms

When the direct object pronoun (*o, a, os, as*) is
attached to conjugated verbs, it changes form slightly to *lo,
la, los,* and *las.* See the following examples:

Você quer experimentar a torta?
Do you want to try the pie?

*Sim, quero experiment**á-la**.*
Yes, I want to try **it**.

Ela vai ler as revistas?
Is she going to read the magazines?

*Sim, ela vai lê-**las**.*
Yes, she is going to read **them**.

Vocês gostariam de ouvir meu disco?
Would you all like to hear my album?

*Sim, gostaríamos de ouv**i-lo**.*
Yes, we like to listen to **it**.

Notice that you most drop the *–r* ending of the infinitive and add an accent (from *ar* to *á*, and from *er* to *ê*). The infinitives that end in *ir* remain as *i*.

Indirect Object Pronouns

The indirect object tells for whom or to whom an action is done. It also replaces a noun in a sentence. If you say, "I gave the passport to Mário," someone can say, "Why did you give the passport to him?" in which case "him" is the indirect object pronoun that is replacing the proper noun "Mário." Here is a list of indirect object pronouns in Brazilian Portuguese:

INDIRECT OBJECT PRONOUNS	
me	to/for me
te	to/for you (sing. informal)
lhe	to/for you (sing. formal), him, her, it
nos	to/for us
lhes	to/for you (plural), them

Some verbs have two objects; that is, they have a direct as well as an indirect object. Verbs such as "to give" or "to offer" or "to deliver" imply that <u>something</u> was done to <u>someone</u>. Here's a list of these common "double-pronoun" verbs.

DOUBLE-PRONOUN VERBS	
dar	to give
dever	to owe
emprestar	to lend
entregar	to deliver
ensinar	to teach
enviar	to send
explicar	to explain
mandar	to send
oferecer	to offer
perguntar	to ask a question
recomendar	to recommend
telefonar	to call, telephone

Here are some examples of how the indirect object pronoun works in Brazilian Portuguese.

*O oficial **me** deu o visto.*
The official gave the visa **to me**.

*Eu **te** falei muitas coisas.*
I told lots of things **to you**.

*Ela vai **nos** ligar?*
She is going to call **us**?

*Os meninos? Nós **lhes** telefonamos.*
The boys? We called **them**.

*A professora? Eu **lhe** entreguei a tarefa.*
The professor? I gave the work **to her**.

In some instances, the indirect object pronoun system is not used and the preposition *para* is used instead. Read the following sentences, which are equivalent to the previous two sentences.

*Os meninos? Nós telefonamos **para eles**.*
oohs meh-nee-noos NOYS teh-leh-fohn-nahn-moos
pah-ra EH-lees

*A professora? Eu entreguei a tarefa **para ela**.*
Ah proh-feh-SSO-rah Eh-oo ehn-treh-gay ah tah-reh-fah
pah-ra EH-lah

Reflexive and Reciprocal Verbs and Pronouns

Reflexive verbs indicate that the subject of a sentence is performing the action of the verb on himself/herself/itself. They can be translated to English by using the reflexive pronouns "-self" and "-selves," as in *eu me chamo* "I call myself." Reciprocal verbs can be translated to English by using the construction "each other." In this case, the action is done to an entity, which in turn does the same action to the other entity, as in the expression *se beijam* "they kiss each other." In Portuguese, reflexive and reciprocal verbs are conjugated by using reflexive pronouns.

REFLEXIVE AND RECIPROCAL PRONOUNS

PRONOUN	ENGLISH
eu **me** *chamo*	I call myself
você **se** *chama*	you call yourself
ele/ela **se** *chama*	he/she calls him/herself
nós **nos** *chamamos*	we call ourselves
vocês **se** *chamam*	you all call yourselves
eles/elas **se** *chamam*	they call themselves

Notice that the pronoun is placed before the verb and that pronouns are used for both reflexive and reciprocal ideas.

Alert

Not all reflexive verbs in Portuguese have a corresponding English reflexive verb. The example *chamar-se* "to call oneself" works well, but other reflexive verbs in Portuguese are non-reflexive in English. For example, *levantar-se* "to get up" is not considered reflexive in English.

Here is a list of common reflexive verbs in Portuguese:

COMMON REFLEXIVE VERBS

VERB	ENGLISH
lavar-se	to wash oneself
vestir-se	to put on clothes, to dress oneself
olhar-se	to look at oneself
pentear-se	to brush/comb oneself

COMMON REFLEXIVE VERBS (*CONTINUED*)

VERB	ENGLISH
sentar-se	to sit oneself
divertir-se	to entertain oneself, to have fun
deitar-se	to go to bed, to retire
machucar-se	to hurt oneself
reunir-se	to get together

In order to conjugate the verb, you must drop the *-se* and add one of the reflexive pronouns according to the grammatical person. So *deitar-se* would be conjugated as *eu **me** deito* "I go to bed" in the first person singular.

Useful Reflexive Verbs

Some reflexive verbs are often used with prepositions and/or other verbs. Here's a list of these verbs.

REFLEXIVE VERBS (*-SE*) WITH PREPOSITIONS (*DE, A, COM*)

VERB	ENGLISH
*aproveitar-se **de***	to take advantage of
*convencer-se **de***	to convince oneself of
*esquecer-se **de***	to forget to (plus a verb in infinitive)
*lembrar-se **de***	to remember to (plus a verb in infinitive)
*queixar-se **de***	to complain about
*rir-se **de***	to laugh at
*decidir-se **a***	to decide to (plus a verb in infinitive)
*dedicar-se **a***	to dedicate oneself to
*acostumar-se **com***	to get used to
*parecer-se **com***	to look like
*casar-se **com***	to marry

VERB	ENGLISH
preocupar-se **com**	to worry about
surpreender-se **com**	to be surprised

Notice that not all verbs are translated with a preposition. In English "to forget to" is followed by another verb in English, as in "to forget to add a sentence." However, in Portuguese, that verb is reflexive (*-se* ending) and is followed by the preposition *a* "to." Careful: the same preposition can be translated as "at," "about," or "with." Also, some verbs such as "to marry" and "to be surprised" do not require a preposition at all in English.

Adjectives and Gender

An adjective is a word that modifies or describes a noun (a delicious dish, an outgoing person). In English, all adjectives come before the noun. In Portuguese, most adjectives follow the noun that they modify, although there is a category of commonly used adjectives that precede nouns.

Portuguese adjectives must agree in gender and number with the nouns that they modify. That is, if a noun is masculine plural (*livros* [books], for example), the adjective that modifies it must be masculine and plural as well (*livros caros* [expensive books]). This means that there can be up to four forms of each adjective: masculine singular, feminine singular, masculine plural, and feminine plural.

EXAMPLES OF DESCRIPTIVE NOUN PHRASES

PORTUGUESE	ENGLISH
*o livro **caro***	the **expensive** book
*os livros **caros***	the **expensive** books
*a bolsa **cara***	the **expensive** bag
*as bolsas **caras***	the **expensive** bags

 Alert

Don't forget that nouns have a number (singular or plural) and a gender (masculine or feminine), often indicated by the ending of the word: the letter *-a* is generally feminine, *-o* masculine, and *-s* indicates plurality, with a few exceptions (as mentioned earlier). When the adjective ends in *-e*, there is no difference between the masculine and feminine forms: *um documento importante* (masc.) "an important document" or *uma pessoa importante* (fem.) "an important person."

Possessive, Demonstrative, and Interrogative Adjectives

Possessive, demonstrative, and interrogative adjectives all precede the nouns they modify.

- Possessive adjectives: *meu* (my), *teu* (your), *seu* (his, her, your), *nosso* (our), etc.
- Demonstrative adjectives: *este* (this), *esse* (that), *aquele* (the one over there), etc.
- Interrogative adjectives: *qual, quais* (which)

Adjectives That Precede the Noun

Almost all adjectives follow the noun that they modify, but there are exceptions to that rule. The following is a group of commonly used adjectives that precede the noun they modify.

PORTUGUESE ADJECTIVE	ENGLISH EQUIVALENT
outro/outra OH-troo/OH-trah	another
belo/bela BEH-loh/BEH-lah	beautiful
bom/boa bohn/BOH-ah	good
jovem JOH-vehn	young
grande GRAHN-dee	large; great
longo/longa LON-goo/LON-gah	long
novo/nova NOH-voh/NOH-vah	new
pequeno/pequena PEE-keh-noo/PEE-keh-nah	small; little
mesmo/mesma MEHS-moo/MEHS-mah	same
velho/velha VEH-lyo/VEH-lya	old

Fact

In some cases, an adjective can come either before or after the noun it modifies. In these cases, the meaning of the adjective can change. For example, *um novo carro* = a new car (a car I just bought, could be old, but new to me), but *um carro novo* = a new car (a car made this year).

Some Useful Adjectives for Describing Yourself

Almost all adjectives follow the noun that they modify. The following is a group of commonly used adjectives that follow this rule.

PORTUGUESE ADJECTIVE	ENGLISH EQUIVALENT
louro/loura LOW-roo/LOW-rah	blonde
moreno/morena moh-REHN-noo/moh-REHN-nah	dark-skinned
alto/alta AHL-toh/AHL-tah	tall
baixo/baixa BAH-ee-shoo/BAH-ee-shah	short
magro/magra MAH-groo/MAH-grah	slender; skinny
gordo/gorda GOR-doo/GOR-dah	fat

feio/feia	ugly
FAY-yoo/FAY-yah	
rico/rica	rich
HEE-koo/HEE-kah	
pobre	poor
POH-breh	
inteligente	intelligent
en-tehl-lee-JEHN-tee	
estúpido/estúpida	stupid
ehs-TOO-pee-doo/ehs-TOO-pee-dah	
simpático/simpática	kind
seem-PAH-tee-koo/seem-PAH-tee-kah	
antipático/antipática	unpleasant
ahn-tee-PAH-tee-koo/ahn-tee-PAH-tee-kah	
generoso/generosa	generous
jehn-neh-ROH-zoo/jehn-neh-ROH-zah	
chato/chata	boring
SHAH-too/SHAH-tah	
feliz	happy
feh-LEES	
triste	sad
TREES-teh	

Adverbs

Adverbs describe when, how, and where an action is completed. They modify verbs, adjectives, and even other adverbs. In Portuguese, adverbs typically come after the verb that they modify. Some expressions such as *amanhã* (tomorrow), *sempre* (always), and *nunca* (never) are adverbs that indicate "when" things happen. You can also express how you feel with an adverb: *bem* (well) and *mal* (badly). Most adverbs are the so-called "adverbs of manner," which tell "how" things are done. Here are some common examples:

COMMON ADVERBS OF MANNER	
assim ah-SEEN	like that; thus
bem BEH--een	well
mal MAH-oo	badly
rapidamente hah-pee-dah-MEHN-tee	fast
devagar djee-vah-GAH	slowly
melhor meh-LEE-OH	better
pior pee-OH	worse
raramente hah-rah-MEHN-tee	rarely

In English, to create an adverb from an adjective, you add "-ly." In Portuguese, you add *-mente* to the feminine form of the adjective, as in *rápido* > *rápida* > *rapidamente* (rapidly, fast). Remember to drop the accent when you change to an adverb. Not all adverbs follow this rule; some have altogether different forms such as the adjective *bom* (good) and the comparative adverb *melhor* (better).

Adverbs of Place

These adverbs indicate the place where something happens. Here are some examples:

COMMON ADVERBS OF PLACE	
aqui	here
ah-KEE	
ali	over there
ah-LEE	
atrás	behind
ah-TRAHSS	
lá	over there
LAH	
perto	near
PEHR-too	
defronte	facing
deh-FROHN-tee	
dentro	inside
DEHN-troo	
debaixo	under; below
dee-BAH-EE-shoo	
embaixo	below; under
ehn-BAH-EE-shoo	
longe	far
LOHN-jee	

Adverbs of Time

There are also some adverbs that relate to time, or when actions are done. Here is a list.

COMMON ADVERBS OF TIME	
agora ah-GOH-rah	now
amanhã ah-MAHN-nee-AHN	tomorrow
antes AHN-tees	before
ainda ah-EEN-dah	yet
cedo SEH-doo	early
depois deh-POH-ees	after; then
então en-TAHN-oo	then
hoje OH-jee	today
já JAH	now; already
logo LOH-goo	soon
nunca NOOHN-kah	never
ontem OHN-tehn-ee	yesterday

COMMON ADVERBS OF TIME (*CONTINUED*)	
sempre SEHN-pree	always
tarde TAHR-dee	late

Adverbs of Quantity

Adverbs of quantity express how much or how many are related to the adjective or the verb. These are the common adverbs of quantity in Portuguese:

COMMON ADVERBS OF QUANTITY	
bastante bas-TAHN-tee	enough; rather
quase KWA-zee	almost
demais dee-MAH-ees	too much
mais MAH-ees	more
menos MEH-noos	less; fewer
muito MOO-yeen-too	a lot
pouco POH-koo	a little
somente saw-MEHN-tee	only

COMMON ADVERBS OF QUANTITY (*CONTINUED*)

tão	as
TAHN-oo	
tanto	so (much)
TAHN-too	

The following are some examples of adverbs that modify verbs and adjectives:

*Nós comemos **demais**!*	We ate **too much**!
*Ele **quase** ficou doente.*	He **almost** got sick.
*Eles estão **muito** cansados.*	They are **very** tired.
*Eu estou **bastante** estressada!*	I am **pretty** stressed out!

Unlike adjectives, adverbs do not change. Note that the adverb *muito* "very" is an invariable form that modifies a verb. The same word can be a variable adjective that modifies a noun, such as *muitos exercícios* "many exercises" and *muitas atividades* "many activities."

CHAPTER 3

Essential Brazilian Portuguese

There are certain vocabulary words and expressions that will prove more useful to you as a traveler in Brazil. Aside from the common phrases like "Do you speak English?" and "Where are you from?" it is important to understand the differences between formal and informal speech. In addition, knowing the basics such as numbers, days of the week, the calendar, and how to tell time is crucial for successful communication.

Survival Brazilian Portuguese

Take a look at the following Portuguese phrases—they will come in handy as you begin communicating in this language.

I don't speak Portuguese very well.
Não falo português muito bem.
NAHN-oo FAH-loo pooh-too-GA-ees -MOO-yeen-too BEH-een

Could you repeat, please?
Pode repetir, por favor?
POH-dee heh-peh-TEEH poh fah-VOH

Can you speak more slowly?
Pode falar mais devagar?
POH-dee fah-LAH MAH-ees dee-vah-GAH

I don't understand.
Não entendo.
NAHN-oo ehn-TEHN-doo

Do you speak English?
Você fala inglês?
voh-SAY FAH-lah een-GLAY-ees

What does . . . mean?
O que quer dizer . . . ?
OOH kee kher dee-ZEH . . .

How do you say . . . in Portuguese?
Como se diz . . . em portugués?
KOH-moo see djees . . . ehn pohr-too-GEH-yees

Language Basics

In order to have any basic conversation in Portuguese, you need to know the following words. Learning how to say yes and no and the valuable question words—who, what, when, where, and why—will help get any conversation started!

yes	*sim*	SEEN
no	*não*	NAHN-oo
okay	*tá bom*	TAH-bohn
and	*e*	ee
or	*ou*	oh
who	*quem*	KEHN-ee
what	*o que*	oo-KEH
when	*quando*	KWAHN-doo
where	*onde*	OHN-dee
why	*por quê*	pohr-KEH
how	*como*	KOH-moo

Being Polite

In Brazilian Portuguese formality can be subtle, as opposed to European Portuguese, where there are clear distinctions between the use of the pronoun *tu* and *você*. In Brazil, it is common to use *o senhor* "Sir" or "Mr." and *a senhora* "Ma'am" or "Mrs." when addressing people in a more formal context.

It might be difficult to decide when the formal way of speaking should be used. As a general rule, use the more formal when meeting people for the first time, when greeting elders, and in business situations. Brazilians will very often immediately tell you when it's time to use the more informal *você*, which will be the majority of the time. That said, for the casual traveler, the following "polite" words will go a long way!

please	*por favor, por gentileza*
	pohr FAH-vohr; pohr jehn-tee-LEH-zah
thank you	*obrigado/obrigada* (male/female speaker)
	oh-bree-GAH-doh/oh-bree-GAH-dah
thank you very much	*muito obrigado/obrigada* (male/female speaker)
	MOO-yeen-too oh-bree-GAH-doh/oh-bree-GAH-dah
you're welcome	*De nada; Imagina!* (slang, very common)
	dee-NAH-dah; ee-mah-GEE-nah
it's my pleasure	*o prazer é todo meu*
	oo prah-ZEH eh TOH-doo MEH-oo
pardon me	*com licença*
	KOHN lee-SEHN-sah
I'm sorry	*Desculpa*
	dehs-KOOL-pah

TITLES	
sir; Mr.	*senhor*
	sehn-nee-OH
ma'am; Mrs.	*senhora*
	sehn-nee-OH-rah

 Alert

It is very important to note that, more commonly, you will hear *Seu* for "Mr." and *Dona* for "Mrs." followed by one's first name, as in *Seu Amilcar* (Mr. Amilcar) and *Dona Marta* (Mrs. Marta).

Numbers 1 Through 100 and Beyond

What's the number of the bus we should take? What time is it? How much is this scarf? Knowing numbers will better prepare you to understand the responses to these questions!

NUMBERS 1 TO 100	
1	*um/uma*
	OOHN/OOHN-ah
2	*dois/duas*
	DOH-ees/DOO-ahs
3	*três*
	TREH-ees
4	*quatro*
	KWAH-troo

NUMBERS 1 TO 100 (*CONTINUED*)

5	*cinco*	
	SEEN-koo	
6	*seis*	
	SAY-eesh	
7	*sete*	
	SEH-tee	
8	*oito*	
	OY-too	
9	*nove*	
	NOH-vee	
10	*dez*	
	DEH-ees	
11	*onze*	
	OHN-zee	
12	*doze*	
	DOH-zee	
13	*treze*	
	TREH-zee	
14	*catorze*	
	kah-TOHR-zee	
15	*quinze*	
	KEEN-zee	
16	*dezesseis*	
	deh-zeh-SAY-eesh	
17	*dezessete*	
	deh-zeh-SEH-tee	
18	*dezoito*	
	deh-ZOY-too	

NUMBERS 1 TO 100 (*CONTINUED*)

19	*dezenove*	
	deh-zeh-NOH-vee	
20	*vinte*	
	VEEN-tee	
21	*vinte e um*	
	VEEN-tee ee oohn	
22	*vinte e dois*	
	VEEN-tee ee DOH-eesh	
30	*trinta*	
	TREEN-tah	
40	*quarenta*	
	kwah-REHN-tah	
50	*cinquenta*	
	seen-KWEHN-tah	
60	*sessenta*	
	seh-SEHN-tah	
70	*setenta*	
	seh-TEHN-tah	
80	*oitenta*	
	oy-TEHN-tah	
90	*noventa*	
	noh-VEHN-tah	
100	*cem*	
	SEHN-ee	

LARGER NUMBERS

1,000	*mil*
	MEEL
1,200	*mil e duzentos*
	meel ee doo-ZEHN-toos
2,000	*dois mil/duas mil*
	DOH-ees meel/DOO-ahs meel
5,000	*cinco mil*
	SEEN-koo meel
10,000	*dez mil*
	DEH-eesh meel
100,000	*cem mil*
	SEHN-ee meel
1,000,000	*um milhão*
	OHN mee-lyahn-oo
1,000,000,000	*um bilhão*
	OHN bee-lyahn-oo

 Essential

All numbers are invariable as far as gender except for *um/uma* and *dois/duas*, since they both have a masculine and a feminine form. *Um*, you may notice, has the same forms as the indefinite article "a/an." This means that if you say *um cliente* you could mean "a client" or "one client," depending on the context.

Fact

Understanding the written-out numerals in Portuguese can be tricky. Portuguese speakers use a decimal point where a comma would be used in the United States, and vice versa. So the American 1,200 would be written as 1.200, and the American 1.5 (as in one and a half) would be written as 1,5 in Brazil.

 **Essential**

The common abbreviations used for ordinal numbers (1st, 2nd, and 3rd) are different in Portuguese, as can be expected. When expressing abbreviated ordinal numbers, use the superscripts 1° (*primeiro*) or 1ª (*primeira*) depending on the gender of the noun. Use the same symbols for all sequences, 2° (*segundo*) and 2ª (*segunda*), and so on.

Telling Time

Telling time in Portuguese differs greatly from telling time in English. You might have to check in to the hotel by 14h and attend a play at 21h30. Brazilians use the 24-hour clock or the so-called "military time" to track the hours in a day. When time is expressed numerically, the number of hours is written followed by a lower case letter *h*, after which the number of minutes is written. It can be tricky, but the following guide will save you from missing your important appointments! Until midday or noon, say *da manhã*. For example, *onze horas da manhã* means "eleven in the morning." To say it is twelve past noon, use *da tarde*, as in *uma hora da tarde* or "one in the afternoon." Finally, as soon as the sun sets, use *da noite*. This means that around 6 P.M., depending if it's still light outside, you can say *seis horas da tarde* "six in the afternoon," or if it's dark outside, you should say *seis horas da noite*, "six in the evening."

What time is it?	*Que horas são?*
	keh OH-rah SAHN-oo
It's 8:30.	*São oito e trinta.*
	sahn-oo OY-toh ee TREEN-tah

The plural verb *são* is used to express the time that is 2:00 P.M. and beyond. The singular verb *é* is used to express the time between 1:00 P.M. and 1:59 P.M.

It's 1:00.	*É uma hora.*
	eh OOHN-ah oh-ra
It's 1:10.	*É uma e dez.*
	eh OOHN-ah ee DEH-eesh
It's 1:45.	*É uma e quarenta e cinco.*
	eh OOHN-ah ee kwah-REHN-tah e SEEN-koo

🆘 Alert

You don't need to specify P.M. or A.M. when saying the time in Portuguese, when it is obvious to the speaker (i.e. the conversation context will tell you if it's in the middle of the afternoon or the morning). However, if you are unsure and you need to clarify, use one of the following expressions: *da manhã* "in the morning," *da tarde* "in the afternoon," or *da noite* "in the evening."

And *É . . .* is used with the following time expressions:

It's noon.	*É meio-dia.*
	eh MAY-oo-DEE-ah
It's midnight.	*É meia-noite.*
	eh MAY-yah-NOY-tee

The expression *São . . .* is used to express all times from 2:00 P.M. on:

It's 12:20	*São doze e vinte*
	sahn-oo DOH-zee ee VEEN-tee
It's 2:00	*São duas*
	sahn-oo DOO-ahs
It's 3:15	*São três e quinze*
	SAHN-oo treh-zee KEEN-zee
It's 4:30	*São quatro e meia*
	SAHN-oo KWAH-troo ee MAY-yah
It's 4:42	*São quatro e quarenta e dois*
	SAHN-oo KWAH-troo ee kwah-REHN-tah ee DOH-ees

It's 5:05	*São cinco e cinco*
	SAHN-oo SEEN-koo ee SEEN-koo
It's 6:55	*São cinco para as sete*
	sahn-oo SEEN-koo pah-ra ahs SEH-tchee
It's 7:45	*São quinze para as oito*
	SAHN-oo KEEN-zee pah-rah ahs OY-too
It's 8 A.M.	*São oito da manhã*
	SAHN-oo OY-too dah manh-ny-AHN
It's 5 P.M.	*São cinco da tarde*
	SAHN-oo SEEN-koo dah TAHR-dee
It's 10 P.M.	*São dez da noite*
	SAHNoo DEY-eesh dah NOY-tee

Fact

In Brazil, the twenty-four-hour clock is commonly used for scheduling purposes. Expect to see it when you look at bus or flight schedules, conference schedules, cinema and television programming, and so on.

The Calendar

The Brazilian calendar begins with Monday and ends with the weekend. Makes sense, right? The weekend is considered Saturday and Sunday. The days of the week, months of the year, and names of seasons are not capitalized in Brazilian Portuguese unless, of course, they are at the beginning of the sentence. This is not the same in Portugal, where they are capitalized always.

DAYS OF THE WEEK

DAY	PORTUGUESE	ENGLISH
Sunday	**domingo** doo-MEEN-goo	"Day of the Lord"
Monday	**segunda-feira** seh-GOON-dah FEY-rah	"Second Holy Day"
Tuesday	**terça-feira** TEHR-sah FEY-rah	"Third Holy Day"
Wednesday	**quarta-feira** KWAHR-tah FEY-rah	"Fourth Holy Day"
Thursday	**quinta-feira** KEEN-tah FEY-rah	"Fifth Holy Day"
Friday	**sexta-feira** SAYS-tah FEY-rah	"Sixth Holy Day"
Saturday	**sábado** SAH-bah-doo	"The Sabbath"

 Essential

To form the plural of the days of the week, you should add an **-s** to both parts of the word, so **segundas-feiras** "Mondays" and **quartas-feiras** "Wednesdays." Also, in spoken Portuguese, it is very common to drop the word *-feira* and simply say *Eu estudo português nas* **terças** *e* **quintas** "I study Portuguese on **Tuesdays** and **Thursdays**."

This distinctive way of expressing weekdays in Portuguese came about because of a very influential bishop known as Martinho de Braga (Portugal). He considered it undignified for good Christians to say the names of weekdays by their original pagan names (*Lunae dies* "Day of the Moon," *Martis dies* "Day of Mars," *Mercurii dies* "Day of Mercury," *Jovis dies* "Day of Jovis or Jupiter," *Veneris dies* "Day of Venus," *Saturni dies* "Day of Saturn," and *Solis dies* "Day of the Sun"). Therefore, starting from Sunday, he devised the names *Prima Feria, Secunda Feria,* etc., meaning "first day," "second day," etc., for the days of the Holy Week. The current word *feira* is a linguistic interpretation of *feria*, which meant "Holy Day" or holiday, a day in which people should not work. Later, the first day (*Prima Feria*) or Sunday, was changed to *Domenica*, which is Latin for the "Day of the Lord." This meaning is also kept in Spanish, Italian, and French.

THE MONTHS

PORTUGUESE	ENGLISH
janeiro jahn-NEY-roo	January
fevereiro feh-veh-REY-roo	February
março MAHR-sue	March
abril ah-BREE-oo	April
maio MAH-yoo	May
junho JOON-nyoo	June

PORTUGUESE	ENGLISH
julho joo-LYOO	July
agosto ah-GOSS-too	August
setembro seh-TENH-broo	September
outubro oo-TOO-broo	October
novembro noh-VENH-broo	November
dezembro deh-ZENH-broo	December

 Essential

When writing the dates in short form, Brazilians start with the day followed by the month and year. So, **9/5** is May 9th, or *nove de maio*, not September 5th! This is of course not a problem with dates after the 12th, since beyond that number, the number can only relate to a day, not a month: **26/07** can only be *vinte e seis de julho* or July 26th. When filling out forms with your birth date, make sure you know where to indicate the day and the month.

THE SEASONS IN BRAZIL

o verão ooh veh-RAHN-oo	the summer	*dezembro, janeiro, fevereiro*
o outono ooh oo-TOH-noo	the fall	*março, abril, maio*

THE SEASONS IN BRAZIL (*CONTINUED*)

o inverno ooh een-VEHR-noo	the winter	*junho, julho, agosto*
a primavera ah pree-mah-VEH-rah	the spring	*setembro, outubro, novembro*

Since parts of Brazil are very tropical, the changing of the seasons is not nearly as evident as it is in countries such as the United States or Canada. In fact, sometimes in the northeast of Brazil, there is only a raining or monsoon season, followed by a drought or dry season. When traveling abroad to countries below the equator, always check with the available online resources to find out which "season" they are in.

CHAPTER 4

Meeting People

One of the first things you may want to do as a traveler is to greet people in their native language. It shows appreciation for the culture and the language. There are many different kinds of ice breakers, or adjectives and expressions, that you can use to start conversations and describe yourself. In the following sections, you will see some verbs in the present tense, nouns, articles, adjectives, as well as pronouns to help you during your travels. Additionally, you will learn some common language used when making telephone calls in Brazil.

Greetings and Introductions

This section introduces you to some valuable expressions that you can use to greet people and start a conversation. Remember, when introducing yourself, be confident and polite!

Ice Breakers

Here are some of the most common phrases you will hear and use during your travels:

Good morning.
Bom dia.
BOHN dee-ah.

Good evening.
Boa noite.
BOAH noy-tee

Hi! (informal)
Oi!
OYE

 Alert

The greeting *Oi* is considered to be very informal. You would use it with friends, but be careful using it in other, more formal situations. You would not use it, for example, in a formal business meeting when addressing potential business partners. In this case you should say *Olá* or *Como vai?* "How are you?"

Conversation Starters

Once you get past the greetings, you may want to get the conversation rolling. Here are some useful conversation starters.

How are you?	*Como vai?*
	KOH-moo VAH-ee?
Fine, thanks.	*Bem, obrigado.*
	BEH-ee oh-bree-GAH-doo
Excellent!	*Ótimo!*
	OH-tee-moh
Yes	*Sim*
	SEEN
No	*Não*
	NAHN-oo
My name is . . .	*Meu nome é . . .*
	meh-oo NOM-ee EH
What's your name?	*Como você se chama?*
	KOH-moo voh-SAY see SHAH-mah?
His name is . . .	*O nome dele é . . .*
	oo NOH-mee DEH-lee EH . . .
Her name is . . .	*O nome dela é . . .*
	oo NOH-mee DEH-lah EH
I am . . .	*Sou . . .*
	SOH-oo . . .
Where are you from?	*De onde você é?*
	dee OHN-dee voh-SAY EH?
I am from the United States	*Sou dos Estados Unidos*
	SOH-oo doos ehs-TAH-doo-zoo-NEE-doos

... from England	... *da Inglaterra*
	... dah een-glah-TEH-hah
... from Australia	... *da Austrália*
	... dah ahs-oos-TRAH-lyah
... from Canada	... *do Canadá*
	... doo kah-nah-DAH
... from France	... *da França*
	... dah FRAHN-sah
... from Spain	... *da Espanha*
	... dah ehs-PAHN-nyah
... from China	... *da China*
	... dah SHEE-nah
... from Japan	... *do Japão*
	... doo jah-PAHN-oo
Thank you	*Obrigado/Obrigada*
	oh-bree-GAH-doo/oh-bree-GAH-dah
Please	*Por favor*
	pohr fah-VOH
You're welcome	*De nada*
	dee NAH-dah
You're welcome!	*Imagina!* (slang, very common)
	ee-mah-GEE-nah
Don't worry about it!	*Não há de que!*
	NAHN-oo ah dee KEH
Nice to meet you.	*Muito prazer.*
	MOO-een-too prah-ZEH
Bye!	*Tchau!*
	CHOW
Goodbye (for good).	*Adeus.*
	ah-DEH-oos

See you later.	*Até mais.*
	ah-TEH MAH-eesh
See you tomorrow.	*Até amanhã.*
	ah-TEH ah-MAHN-nee-AHN
See you next week.	*Até semana que vem.*
	ah-TEH seh-MAHN-nah kee VEHN
See you in a bit.	*Até daqui a pouco.*
	ah-TEH dah-kee ah poh-koo
See you later.	*Até mais tarde.*
	ah-TEH MAH-ees TAHR-dee
Do you speak . . . ?	*Você fala . . . ?*
	voh-SAY FAH-lah
. . . English?	*. . . inglês?*
	een-GLAYS
. . . German?	*. . . alemão?*
	ah-leh-MAHN-oo
. . . French?	*. . . francês?*
	franh-SAYS
. . . Spanish?	*. . . espanhol?*
	ees-pahn-nee-OH-oo
Where is . . . ?	*Onde é . . . ?*
	OHN-dee EH
Can you tell me . . . ?	*Você pode me dizer . . . ?*
(informal)	voh-SAY POH-dee meedee-ZEH
Can you tell me . . . ?	*O senhor/A senhora pode me dizer . . . ?*
(formal)	oo-SEHN-nyoh/
	ah-SEHN-nyOH-rah POH-dee mee–dee-ZEH
Can you show me . . . ?	*Você pode me mostrar . . . ?*
(informal)	voh-SAY POH-dee mee mohs-TRAH

Can you show me . . . ?	*O senhor/*
(formal)	*A senhora pode me mostrar . . . ?*
	oo-SEHN-nyoh/
	ah-SEHN-nyOH-rah POH-dee mee mohs-TRAH
Where is the [place]	*Onde fica o/a [place]?*
located?	OHN-dee FEE-kah oo/ah [place]

Nationalities and Languages

Brazil is a major tourist attraction for people from all over the world. Whether you arrive at the Rio de Janeiro or São Paulo airport in the south, or touch down in one of the northeastern airports of Recife or Fortaleza, you can expect to meet travelers from just about any country in the world. Talking about where you are from and asking where other people are from is a good way to practice your Portuguese. The following is a list of adjectives in the masculine and feminine forms.

 Fact

Adjectives denoting nationality are not capitalized in Portuguese. "I am American" is *Sou americano*, or *Sou americana*. Adjectives also follow the agreement patterns for plural nouns: *Os brasileiros* and *Os cabo-verdianos* mean "The Brazilians" and "The Cape Verdeans," respectively.

I AM . . .	SOU . . . (SOO . . .)
African	*africano/africana*
	ah-free-KANH-noh/ah-free-KANH-nah
American	*americano/americana*
	ah-meh-ree-KANH-noo/ah-meh-ree-KANH-nah
Australian	*australiano/australiana*
	ous-trah-LYAH-noo/ous-trah-LYAH-nah
Belgian	*belgo/belga*
	BEHL-goo/BEHL-gah
Brazilian	*brasileiro/brasileira*
	brah-zee-LAY-roo/brah-zee-LAY-rah
Canadian	*canadense*
	kanh-nah-DEN-see
Chinese	*chinês/chinesa*
	shee-NAYS/shee-NAY-zah
Dutch	*holandês/holandesa*
	oh-lahn-DAYS/oh-lahn-DEH-zah
English	*inglês/inglesa*
	een-GLAYS/een-GLEH-za
European	*europeu/européia*
	eh-oo-roh-PEH-oo/eh-oo-roh-PEH-ya
French	*francês/francesa*
	frahn-SAYS/frahn-SEH-zah
German	*alemão/alemã*
	ah-leh-MAWN/ah-leh-MANH
Indian	*indiano/indiana*
	een-dee-ANH-noo/een-dee-ANH-nah
Irish	*irlandês/irlandesa*
	eer-lahn-DAYS/eer-lahn-DEH-zah

Italian	*italiano/italiana*
	ee-tah-LYAH-noo/ee-tah-LYAH-nah
Japanese	*japonês/japonesa*
	jahp-poh-NAYS/jahp-poh-NEH-zah
Mexican	*mexicano/mexicana*
	meh-shee-KAHN-noh/meh-shee-KAHN-nah
New Zealander	*neo-zelandês/neo-zelandesa*
	neh-oh-zeh-lahn-DAYS/neh-oh-zeh-lahn-DEH-zah
Polish	*polonês/polonesa*
	poh-LAHN-nays/poh-lahn-NEH-zah
Portuguese	*português/portuguesa*
	pohr-too-GAYS/pohr-too-GEH-zah
Russian	*russo/russa*
	HOO-soo/HOO-sha
Scottish	*escocês/escocesa*
	ehs-koh-SAYS/ehs-koh-SEH-zah
Spanish	*espanhol/espanhola*
	ehs-pahn-NYOH-oo/ehs-pahn-NYOH-lah
Swedish	*sueco/sueca*
	soo-EH-koo/soo-EH-kah
Swiss	*suíço/suíça*
	soo-EEH-soo/soo-EEH-sah

Family Members

Talking about your family is a natural progression in a conversation about yourself. Here are some words that you will need to talk about your family members.

father; Dad	*pai*; *papai*
	PAH-ee; pah-PAH-ee
mother; Mom	*mãe*; *mamãe*
	MAHN-ee; mahn-MAHN-ee
parents	*os pais*
	oos PAH-ees
brother	*irmão*
	eer-MANH-oo
sister	*irmã*
	eer-MANH
son	*filho*
	FEE-lyoh
daughter	*filha*
	FEE-lyah
grandfather	*avô*
	ah-VOOH
grandmother	*avó*
	ah-VOH
grandparents	*os avós*
	ooh zah-VOHS
grandchildren	*os netos*
	oos NEH-toos
uncle	*tio*
	TEE-oo, CHEE-oo (variable)
aunt	*tia*
	TEE-ah, CHEE-ah (variable)
nephew	*sobrinho*
	soh-BREEN-nyoh
niece	*sobrinha*
	soh-BREEN-nyah

husband	*marido*
	mah-REE-doo
wife	*esposa*
	ehs-POH-zah
fiancé	*noivo*
	NOY-voo
fiancée	*noiva*
	NOY-vah
stepfather	*padrasto*
	pah-DRAHS-too
stepmother	*madrasta*
	mah-DRAHS-tah
cousin	*primo/prima*
	PREE-moo/PREE-mah
brother-in-law	*cunhado*
	koohn-NYAH-doo
sister-in-law	*cunhado*
	koohn-NYAH-dah
father-in-law	*sogro*
	SOH-groo
mother-in-law	*sogra*
	SOH-grah
child	*criança* (both genders)
	kree-ANH-sah
baby	*o/a bebê* (both genders)
	oo/ah beh-BEY
married	*casado/casada*
	kah-zah-doo/kah-zah-dah
single	*solteiro/solteira*
	sohw-TEY-roo/sohw-TEY-rah

divorced	*divorciado/divorciada*
	dee-vohr-see-AH-doo/dee-vohr-see-AH-dah
separated	*separado/separada*
	seh-pah-RAH-doo/seh-pah-RAH-dah
widowed	*viúvo/viúva*
	vee-OOH-voo/vee-OOH-vah

Telephoning to and from Brazil

These instructions will help you navigate the telecommunication system in Brazil. You will learn skills such as being able to place a call to a hotel in Rio as well as confirming reservations at a restaurant.

Calling Brazil from the United States and Canada

To place a call from the United States or Canada, first dial the United States international code, 011, then dial Brazil's country code, 55, then dial the state code (011 for São Paulo, 021 for Rio), and finally dial the number, which is eight digits. For example, if the Brazilian phone number in Rio is 5555-5555, you must dial the following: 011-55-021-5555-5555.

Calling Another Country from Brazil

To place a call to another country from Brazil, first dial long distance code 00, then the country code (1 for the United States and Canada), then the area code and number.

COUNTRY CODES OF OTHER COUNTRIES

United States	1
Canada	1
United Kingdom	44
France	33
Germany	49
Spain	34
Switzerland	41

Placing a Call Within Brazil

Brazilian phone numbers are comprised of an area (state) code (this will be three digits and begins with a zero) and the phone number. Area codes that begin with the number 8 are toll-free. To make a call from one area code to another, you must dial the full area code and then the number. To call within the same area code, you must dial the area code as well.

 Alert

Brazil is only one or two hours ahead of the United States Eastern Standard Time (EST). For example, if it is 12 P.M. in Boston, it is 2:00 P.M. in São Paulo.

Public Phones

Public phones are easy to find. They're literally everywhere. The phone booths are ear-shaped and are usually painted a bright yellow color for easy recognition. They are called *orelhão* or "big ear." You will need to have a phone card (*cartão telefônico*) to pay for the call. Some older phones will only take coins, and some of the newer phones will only take a phone card.

Phone cards can be purchased at airports, bus stations, sometimes bakery/pastry shops, and newsstands. They are available in various denominations.

Emergency Numbers

In the rare instance that you need to get in touch with emergency services, here is how to reach them:

- Emergencies: 128
- Emergencies (local police): 181, to report a crime
- Fire department: 193
- Ambulance: 192
- Crimes against women: 180

 **Essential**

In Brazil, there are special police stations called *Delegacia da Mulher*, which are staffed by female officers. These places came about because women were often victimized and had a difficult time reporting crimes to male officers. The more welcoming atmosphere made it easier for women to report crimes.

Cell Phones

Whether you plan on bringing your cell phone with you or buying one while you're in Brazil, this section will give some valuable pointers.

GSM (Global System for Mobile Communications) is a type of cell phone and network that is used in most countries including Europe (GSM phones are sometimes called world phones because they can be used around the world). Some U.S. cell phone service providers use GSM, but most do not. You will need a GSM phone in Brazil.

Check with your cell phone service provider to determine if yours is a GSM phone. If it is not, world phones can be purchased easily and inexpensively from numerous online vendors. If you have a GSM phone, check with your service provider to determine the costs involved with using your phone while you are abroad. Some companies offer reasonable rates for use abroad, while others are quite expensive.

If your U.S. cellular service provider does not offer international service, it is possible—and often economical—to buy a phone complete with a SIM card from a reputable online source. Waiting until you arrive in Brazil to buy a phone at the airport or from a cell phone store is possible, but could be costly.

SIM Cards

A SIM (Subscriber Information Module) card is a small chip inserted into your phone that contains your cell phone number and your account information. The SIM card can easily be switched from one phone to another. Provided you're in possession of a world phone, it may be possible for you to purchase a SIM card in Brazil and simply use it while you travel. This is a good option all over the world as these cell phone plans do not require lengthy contract commitments. SIM cards come with a certain number of prepaid minutes, and once you've used your minutes, you can either discard the SIM card or purchase more minutes. Also, there is no per-minute charge for incoming calls.

TELEPHONE VOCABULARY	
cell phone	*telefone celular*
	teh-leh-FOHN-nee seh-loo-LAH
reverse charges/collect call	*a pagar*
	ah-pah-GAH
busy	*ocupado*
	oh-koo-PAH-doo
please hold	*aguarde, por favor*
	ah-GWAHR-dee pohr-fah-VOH
to hang up	*desligar*
	dehs-lee-GAH
to call back	*chamar de volta*; *chamar de novo*
	shah-MAH dee VOHL-tah; shah-MAH dee NOH-voo
to ring; it's ringing	*tocar*; *tá tocando*
	toh-CAH; tah-toh-KAHN-doo
telephone	*o telefone*
	oo teh-leh-FOHN-nee
telephone booth	*a cabine telefônica*
	ah kah-BEE-neh teh-leh-FOHN-nee-kah
telephone call	*a chamada*; *o telefonema*
	ah shah-MAH-dah; oo teh-leh-fohn-NEH-mah

TELEPHONE VOCABULARY (*CONTINUED*)

telephone directory	*o guia telefônico*
	oo GHEE-ah teh-leh-FOHN-nee-koo
telephone number	*o número (de telefone)*
	oo NOO-meh-roo (dee teh-leh-FOHN-nee)
dialing tone	*o sinal acústico*
	oo see-NAHL ah-KOOS-tee-koo

CHAPTER 5

Airports and Hotels

You have already been introduced to the essential language structures needed for basic conversation (verbs, adjectives, adverbs, and basic expressions) in order to communicate in Portuguese. The following will build on that foundation and will provide you with practical and useful information you need to be fluent in an airport, a bus station, or a hotel.

Airport and Flight Vocabulary

The hustle and bustle of the airport can be stressful. Knowing the following terms and expressions may help to alleviate some of that stress and help you feel more comfortable.

PEOPLE, PLACES, AND THINGS	
airplane	*o avião*
	oo ah-vee-AHWN-oo
airport	*o aeroporto*
	oo ah-eh-roh-POHR-too
baggage	*a bagagem*
	ah bah-gah-JEYEN
boarding pass	*o cartão de embarque*
	oo kahr-TAWN dee eyn-BAHR-kee
carry-on luggage	*a bagagem de mão*
	ah bah-gah-JEYEN dee MAWHN
checked luggage	*a bagagem despachada*
	ah bah-gah-JEYN dehs-pah-SHAH-dah
cart	*um carrinho*
	oohn-kahr-HEEN-yoo
check-in desk	*o balcão de check-in*
	oo bahw-KAHWN dee cheh-keen
departures	*partidas*
	pahr-TEE-dahs
arrivals	*chegadas*
	sheh-GAH-dahs
early	*antecipado*
	ahn-teh-see-PAH-doo

PEOPLE, PLACES, AND THINGS (CONTINUED)

late	*atrasado*
	ah-trah-ZAH-doo

 Fact

You will notice that some English words are used for terms related to international travel. *A loja duty free* is a duty-free shop and many Brazilians will complete *o check-in,* and so on.

The Verbs *Ir, Vir,* and *Chegar*

Ir means "to go," *chegar* means "to arrive," and *vir* means "to come." They are most useful in the present tense as well as in the past tense. As a traveler, these verbs are very important to know. Here are some sample sentences.

We are going to Rio.
Vamos para o Rio.
VAH-moos PAH-rah oo HEE-oo.

He's coming with us.
Ele vem conosco.
EH-lee vehn ko-NOHS-koo

The plane arrives at seven.
O avião chega às sete.
oo ah-vee-AHN-oo SHEH-gah ahs SEH-tee

PRESENT *IR*	PRESENT *VIR*	PRESENT *CHEGAR*
eu vou	*venho*	*chego*
eh-oo vo	vehn-yoo	sheh-goo
você vai	*vem*	*chega*
voh-seh vah-ee	vehn-ee	sheh-gah
ele/ela vai	*vem*	*chega*
eh-lee/eh-lah vah-ee	vehn-ee	sheh-gah
nós vamos	*vimos*	*chegamos*
noh-ees vah-moos	vee-moos	sheh-GAH-moos
vocês vão	*vêm*	*chegam*
voh-seh-ees vahn-oo	vehn-ee	sheh-gahn-oo
eles/elas vão	*vêm*	*chegam*
eh-lees/eh-lahs vahn-oo	vehn-ee	sheh-gahn-oo

 **Essential**

Both *ir* and *vir* are irregular in the present and past tenses. You will notice that several high frequency verbs have irregular conjugations. Some linguists claim that this is because they have more opportunities to change due to rate of usage.

TICKET INFORMATION

airline	*a companhia aérea*
	ah kom-pah-nee-ya ah-EH-reh-ah
first class	*a primeira classe*
	ah pree-MEY-rah CLAH-ssee
flight	*o vôo*
	oo VOH-oo

TICKET INFORMATION (*CONTINUED*)

gate	*o portão*
	oo pohr-TAWHN-oo
one-way ticket	*uma passagem só de ida.*
	OOHN-ah pah-SAH-jehn-ee-SOH dee EE-dah
round-trip ticket	*uma passagem de ida e volta*
	OOHN-ah pah-SAH-jehn-ee dee EE-dah ee VOHL-tah
terminal	*o terminal*
	oo tehr-mee-NAH-oo

TRAVEL VERBS

to board	*embarcar*
	ehm-BAHR-kah
to buy a ticket	*comprar uma passagem*
	kom-PRAH oohn-ah pah-SAH-jehn-ee
to check bags	*despachar as malas*
	dehs-pah-SHAH ahs MAH-lahs
to make a reservation	*fazer uma reserva*
	fah-zeh oohn-ah reh-ZEHR-vah
to sit down	*sentar, acomodar-se*
	sehn-TAHR; ah-koh-moh-DAHR-see
to take off	*decolar*
	deh-kohl-LAH
to land	*aterrisar*
	ah-teh-hee-ZAH

Baggage Claim, Immigration, and Customs

Before you can enjoy a nice day at the beach in Brazil, you have to get out of the airport. Unfortunately, you have to pass through customs first. The following list of terms will help you get through customs smoothly with no hassles.

ARRIVALS AND BAGGAGE

arrivals	*chegadas*
	sheh-GAH-dahs
baggage claim	*área de bagagem*
	AH-reh-ah dee bah-GAH-jehn
lost luggage	*bagagem extraviada*
	bah-GAH-jehn ehs-trah-vee-AH-dah
My luggage is lost.	*Minha bagagem* (or *minha mala*) *não chegou.*
	meen-nyah bah-GAH-jehn
	(meen-nyah MAH-lah) nahn-oo sheh-GOH

IMMIGRATION AND CUSTOMS

immigration	*imigração*
	ee-mee-grah-SAHN-oo
last name	*sobrenome*
	soh-breh-NOH-mee
first name	*nome*
	NOH-mee
customs	*alfândega*
	ahl-FAHN-deh-gah
nothing to declare	*nada a declarar*
	NAH-dah ah deh-klah-RAH

IMMIGRATION AND CUSTOMS (*CONTINUED*)

customs declaration form   *formulário da aduana*
fohr-moo-LAH-ree-oo dah ah-doo-AH-nah

Here's my passport.
Aqui está meu passaporte.
ah-kee ehsTAH meh-oo pahs-sah-POHR-tee

I have a visa.
Tenho um visto.
TEHN-ee-oo oohn VEES-toh

I don't have a visa.
Não tenho um visto.
NAHN-oo TEHN-ee-oo oohn VEES-toh

I would like to declare …
Gostaria de declarar . . .
gohs-tah-REE-ah dee deh-klah-RAH

 **Essential**

The U.S. Embassy is located in the capital, Brasília. There is a Consulate General in each large Brazilian urban center, such as São Paulo, Rio de Janeiro, and Recife. In addition, there are consulate agencies around the country. These governmental agencies answer telephone calls around the clock and have websites for more information.

Traveling by Bus

It is cheaper to travel by bus in Brazil, although plane tickets have become inexpensive. However, if you would like to experience more of Brazil's countryside, taking a bus is a much better option. Many people travel from São Paulo's *Estação Tietê*, arguably the biggest bus station in the most populated center of Brazil, to cities such as Rio de Janeiro, Niterói, Curitiba, and Belo Horizonte, among others. You should plan on arriving on time and spending four to eight hours on the road, depending on where you are going. Be cognizant of the fact that sometimes there is petty theft in large bus stations, so be aware of your surroundings and keep your money and documents on your person and secure at all times.

BUS VOCABULARY

arrival	*chegada*
	sheh-GAH-dah
driver	*motorista*
	moh-toh-REES-tah
corridor	*corredor*
	koh-heh-DOHR
departure	*partida*
	pahr-TEE-dah
luggage compartment	*compartimento de bagagem*
	kohn-pahr-tee-MEHN-too dee bah-GAH-zhehn
non-smokers	*não fumantes*
	NAHN-oo foo-MAHN-tees

BUS VOCABULARY (CONTINUED)

smokers	*fumantes*	
	foo-MAHN-tees	
reservation	*reserva*	
	heh-ZEHR-vah	
seat	*assento; lugar*	
	ah-SEHN-too; loo-GAH	
station	*estação*	
	ehs-tah-SAHN-oo	
ticket	*passagem*	
	pah-SAH-zhehn-ee	
ticket office	*balcão*	
	bah-KAHN-oo	
toilet; bathroom	*sanitário*	
	sahn-nee-TAH-ree-oo	
validate	*carimbar*	
	kah-reen-BAH	
window	*janela*	
	jah-NEH-lah	

At the Hotel

You're jet-lagged and in need of a nap, a shower, and a bite to eat. All you have is a few *Reais* (Brazilian currency) and this book. The following useful terms and expressions will help satisfy your every need.

I WOULD LIKE A ROOM FOR/WITH . . .
QUERO UM QUARTO POR/COM . . .

one night	*uma noite*
	oohn-ah NOY-tee
two nights	*duas noites*
	DOO-ahs NOY-tees
one person	*uma pessoa*
	oohn-ah peh-SSOH-ah
two people	*duas pessoas*
	DOO-ahs peh-SSOH-ahs
two beds	*duas camas*
	DOO-ahs KAHN-mahs
double bed	*cama de casal*
	KAHN-mah dee kah-ZAH-oo
shower in the room	*com banheiro no quarto*
	kohn bahn-NEEye-roo noo KWAR-too
a bathtub	*uma banheira*
	oohn-ah bahn-NEEye-rah
the toilet	*a bacia sanitária*
	ah bah-SEE-ya sahn-nee-TAH-ree-ya
the television	*a televisão*
	ah teh-leh-VEE-zahnw-oo
the telephone	*o telefone*
	oo teh-leh-FOHN-nee
the air conditioning	*o ar condicionado*
	oo ahr kohn-dee-see-ohn-NAH-doo

IS THERE A(N) . . . ?	TEM UM/UMA . . . ?
elevator	*um elevador*
	oohn eh-leh-vah-DOHR
hairdresser/barber	*um cabeleireiro/um barbeiro*
	oohn kah-beh-ley-RAY-roo/oohn bahr-BAY-roo
parking lot	*um estacionamento*
	oohn ehs-tah-see-oh-nah-MENH-too
restaurant	*um restaurante*
	oohn hehs-tahw-RAHN-tee
pool	*uma piscina*
	oo-nah pee-SHEE-nah

NAVIGATING YOUR HOTEL	
first floor (U.S.); ground floor (Brazil)	*térreo*
	TEH-heh-oo
second floor (U.S.); first floor (Brazil)	*primeiro andar*
	pree-MAY-roo ahn-DAH
hallway	*corredor*
	koh-heh-DOHR
room	*quarto*
	KWAHR-too
door	*porta*
	POHR-tah
window	*janela*
	jah-NEH-lah
bed	*cama*
	KAHN-mah
pillow	*travesseiro*
	trah-vee-SAY-roo

NAVIGATING YOUR HOTEL (CONTINUED)

lamp	*abaju*
	ah-bah-JOO
bathroom	*banheiro*
	bahn-NEE-ye-roo
towel	*toalha*
	toh-AH-lee-ya
wake-up call	*chamada de despertar*
	shah-MAH-dah dee dehs-pehr-TAH

What time is check in/check out?
A que hora é o check-in/o check-out?
ah keh OH-rah EH oo check-EEN/oo check-ow-tee

Is it possible to rent a car?
É possível alugar um carro?
EH poo-SEE-veh-oo ah-loo-GAH oohn KAH-hoo

What do you serve for breakfast here?
O que vocês servem no café da manhã aqui?
oo KEH voh-SAYS SEHR-vehn noo kah-FEH dah
MANH-nyAHN ah-kee

What time is breakfast served?
A que horas começa o café da manhã?
ah kee OH-rahs koh-MEH-ssah oo kah-FEH dah
MANH-nyAHN

Does your hotel have an elevator? A garage?
O hotel tem um elevador? Uma garagem?
oo oh-TEH-oo tehn oohn eh-leh-vah-DOH? oo-nah
gah-RAH-zhehn

Is Internet access available for guests?
Tem serviço de internet para os hóspedes?
tehn sehr-VEE-soo dee ihn-tehr-NEH-tee
PAH-roo-ZOHS-peh-dees

How far away from the hotel is the airport/bus station?
*Qual é a distância do hotel para o aeroporto/a estação
de ônibus?*
KWA-oo EH ah-dees-TAHN-see-ah doo oh-TEH-oo PAH-
rah oo ah-eh-roh-POHR-too/ ah ehs-tah-SAHNW-oo
dee OHN-nee-boos

What's the best way to get to the hotel from
the airport?
*Qual a melhor maneira de ir do aeroporto para
o hotel?*
KWA-oo ah meh-LEE-yoh mahn-NEY-rah dee EER doo
ah-eh-roh-POHR-too PAH-rah oo oh-TEW-oo

How far is the closest bus stop?
Qual a parada de ônibus mais próxima?
KWA-oo ah pah-RAH-dah dee OHN-nee-boos MAH-ees
PROH-see-mah

Can I reserve tickets through the hotel?
É possível comprar os bilhetes aqui no hotel?
EH poh-SEE-veh-oo kohn-PRAH oos-bee-LEEye-teez
ah-kee noo OH-teh-oo

Is the hotel in the historical center of the city?
O hotel está localizado no centro histórico?
oo OH-teh-oo ehs-TAH loh-kah-lee-ZAH-doo noo
SEHN-troo ees-TOH-ree-koo

Settling Your Bill

Sadly, your trip is coming to an end, and now you have
to pay your hotel bill! Here are some useful expressions to
help get your hotel bill settled.

How much is it?
Quanto é?
KWAHN-too EH

I would like to pay my bill.
Gostaria de pagar a conta.
gohs-TAH-ree-ah dee pah-GAH ah KOHN-tah

 Alert

Be sure to ask ahead of time if the hotel takes credit
cards or traveler's checks. Small, family-run hotels might
only accept cash.

I WOULD LIKE TO PAY . . . GOSTARIA DE PAGAR . . .

in cash	*em dinheiro*
	ehn deen-YEH-roo
with traveler's checks	*com travelers check*
	kohn trah-veh-lehrs SHEH-kees
with a credit card	*com cartão de crédito*
	kohn kahr-TAHN-oo dee KREH-dee-too

CHAPTER 6

Getting Around Town

Asking directions, hailing a cab, and reading a bus schedule are all things you might want to know how to do during a trip to Brazil. Make sure that you know where to go and what to ask before venturing out of the hotel. You don't want to get lost and not know how to ask for assistance! The following sections can help you plan your trip as well as give you words so that you may find your way around.

Asking for Directions

Perhaps the most frequently asked questions in all tourist destinations have to do with asking for directions. Here are some useful phrases to ask for help while finding your way around:

Excuse me, where is …?
Com licença, onde fica …?
kohn lee-SEHN-sah ohn-dee-FEE-kah

Please, could you tell me where is …?
Por favor, poderia me dizer onde fica . . . ?
pohr fah-VOH poh-deh-ree-ah mee dee-ZEHR ohn-dee
FEE-kah

Is it very far?
É muito longe?
EH moo-een-too LOHN-jee

How long will it take by car?
Quanto tempo leva de carro?
KWAHN-too TEHN-poo LEH-vah dee KAH-hoo

How far away is the station?
Qual a distância da estação?
KWAH-oo ah dees-TAHN-see-ya dah ehs-tah-SAHN-oo

How much further to …?
Quanto falta . . . ?
KWAHN-too FAH-oo-tah

Excuse me, I'm lost.
Com licença, estou perdido/a.
kohn lee-SEHN-sah ehs-TOH pehr-DEE-doh/-dah

Where is the nearest gas station?
Onde fica o posto de gasolina mais perto?
ohn-dee FEE-kah oo POHS-too dee gah-ZOO-lee-nah
MAH-ees PEHR-too

It's close by.
Fica bem perto.
FEE-kah behn-ee PEHR-too

Can you (sir/ma'am) tell me where it is?
O senhor/A senhora pode me dizer onde fica?
oo sehn-nee-OH/ah sehn-nee-OH-rah POH-dee mee
dee-ZEHR OHN-dee FEE-kah

Can you give me directions to …?
Poderia me dizer como faço para chegar a . . . ?
poh-deh-REE-ya mee dee-ZEHR koh-moo FAH-soo
PAH-rah sheh-GAH ah

DIRECTIONS	
Go straight	*Siga em frente; siga direto*
	SEE-gah ehn FREHN-tee; SEE-gah dee-REH-too
Turn left	*Dobre à esquerda*
	DOH-bree AH eehs-KEHR-dah
Turn right	*Dobre à direita*
	DOH-bree AH dee-REY-tah

DIRECTIONS (CONTINUED)

to the left	*à esquerda*
	AH eehs-KEHR-dah
to the right	*à direita*
	AH dee-REY-tah
straight ahead	*em frente; direto*
	ehn FREHN-tee; dee-REH-too
next to	*perto do/da . . .* (fem. or masc. depending on
	following noun) PEHR-too doo/dah
in front of	*em frente do/da*
	ehn FREHN-tee doo/dah
in back of	*atrás do/da*
	ah-TRAHS doo/dah
near (to)	*próximo a*
	PROH-see-moo AH
far (from)	*longe do/da*
	LOHN-jee doo/dah
north	*norte*
	NOHR-tee
south	*sul*
	SOO
east	*leste*
	LEHS-tee
west	*oeste*
	oh-EHS-tee

Places to Go

This section gives you some useful words related to places found in most cities. Imagine that you left your map at the hotel. How would you communicate your intention of going to the nearest Brazilian restaurant or soccer stadium?

bank	*banco*
	BAHN-koo
bus stop	*parada de ônibus*
	pah-RAH-dah dee OHN-nee-boos
cathedral	*catedral*
	kah-teh-DRAH-oo
church	*igreja*
	ee-GREH-jah
coffee shop; bakery	*padaria*
	pah-dah-REE-ya
garden	*jardin*
	jahr-DEEN
hotel	*hotel; albergue*
	oh-TEH-oo; ah-oo-BEHR-ghee
monument	*monumento*
	moh-noo-MEHN-too
museum	*museu*
	moo-ZEH-oo
open-air market	*mercado*
	mehr-KAH-doo
park	*parque*
	PAHR-kee

restaurant	*restaurante*
	rehs-tah-oo-RAHN-tee
supermarket	*supermercado*
	soo-pehr-mehr-KAH-doo
theater	*teatro*
	teh-AH-troo

Types of Transportation

Big cities in Brazil, such as Rio de Janeiro, São Paulo, and Curitiba, offer a full range of transportation options. Most of these cities have subway systems that are reasonably safe and reliable. For your safety, though, it is important to always be aware of your surroundings and your personal items.

bicycle	*a bicicleta*
	ah bee-see-KLEH-tah
bus	*o ônibus*
	oo OHN-nee-boos
bus stop	*a parada de ônibus*
	ah pah-RAH-dah dee OHN-nee-boos
car	*o carro*
	oo KAH-hoo
motorcycle	*a moto*
	ah MOH-too
subway	*o metrô*
	oo MEH-troh

taxi	*o táxi*
	oo TAHK-see
taxi stand	*a parada de táxi*
	ah pah-RAH-dah dee TAHK-see

Alert

There are usually places in the big cities, near train stations or local town squares, where taxis are all parked waiting for customers. That is called the *parada de taxi*. Look for the first taxi available in the line of cars. More recently, however, taxis have added the call-in service, so you may call their local number and the taxi will pick you up.

Renting a Car

Public transportation and taxis are readily available in all Brazilian cities, but you may want to rent a car to explore off the beaten path. Keep in mind that standard transmissions in cars are the norm in Brazil. If you need a car with an automatic transmission, it is best to make a reservation before you leave for your trip.

I'd like to rent a car.
Gostaria de alugar um carro.
gohs-tah-REE-ya dee ah-loo-GAH oohn KAH-hoo

economy car	*carro classe econômica*
	KAH-hoo KLAH-see eh-koh-NOHN-mee-kah
midsize car	*carro classe intermédia*
	KAH-hoo KLAH-see ihn-tehr-MEH-dee-ah
full-size car	*carro classe full-size*
	KAH-hoo KLAH-see foo-SAH-EE-zee
convertible	*conversível*
	kohn-vehr-SEE-veh-oo
truck	*a pick-up*; *camioneta*
	ah-pee-KAH-pee; ah kah-mee-ohn-NEH-tah
automatic	*automático*
	ahw-toh-MAH-tee-koo

How much will it cost?
Quanto custa?
KWAHN-too KOOS-tah

I'd like to pay by credit card.
Gostaria de pagar com cartão de crédito.
gohs-tah-REE-ah dee pah-GAH kohn kahr-TAHN-oo
dee KREH-dee-too

🅐 Alert

Since 2010, it has become much easier for international
travelers to drive in Brazil. All you need to rent a car is
your valid, original driver's license and a photo ID, such
as your passport.

USEFUL ROAD VOCABULARY

accident	*um acidente*
	oohn ah-see-DEHN-tee
all routes; all directions	*todas as direções*
	TOH-dahz ahs dee-reh-SOHN-yees
bypass road	*estrada de contorno*
	ehs-TRAH-dah dee kohn-TOHR-noo
dead end	*beco sem saída*
	BEH-koo sehn sah-EE-dah
diesel	*o diesel*
	oo DEE-zeh-oo
driver	*o motorista*
	oo moh-toh-REES-tah
gas	*a gasolina*
	ah gah-zoh-LEE-nah
gas station	*o posto de gasolina*
	oo POHS-too dee gah-zoh-LEE-nah
highway	*a auto-estrada*
	ah AH-oo-toh ehs-TRAH-dah
lane	*a faixa*
	ah-FAH-yee-sha
lights	*o farol*
	oo fah-ROH-oo
no parking	*proibido estacionar*
	proh-ee-BEE-doo ehs-tah-see-oh-NAH
no stopping	*proibido parar*
	proh-ee-BEE-doo pah-RAH
one way	*mão única*
	mahn-oo OO-nee-kah

USEFUL ROAD VOCABULARY (*CONTINUED*)

pedestrian	*o pedestre*
	oo peh-DEHS-tree
pedestrian crosswalk	*faixa de pedestre*
	FAH-ee-shah dee peh-DEHS-tree
rush hour	*hora do rush*
	OH-rah doo HUH-shee
speed limit	*limite de velocidade*
	lee-MEE-tee dee veh-loh-see-DAH-dee
stop	*parada*
	pah-RAH-dah
traffic lights	*o semáforo*
	oo seh-MAH-fah-roo

 Alert

Instead of renting a car, it might be a good idea to opt for public transportation in Brazil. Roads in Brazil range from poorly maintained to very well-kept highways. There are significant driving challenges: motorcycles that make their way between cars, pedestrians and stray animals that often cross busy streets, traffic jams, car theft and armed robbery, not to mention aggressive drivers.

Car Talk

Car problems pop up all the time. If, for instance, one of your tires should go flat, you will need to know how to communicate this issue to the correct people. Here are some specific words that you might want to know if you need to communicate about problems with the car.

car	*carro; automóvel*
	KAH-hoo; ahw-toh-MOH-vee-oo
car hood	*o capô*
	oo kah-POH
radio	*o rádio*
	oo HAH-dee-oh
rearview mirror	*o (espelho) retrovisor*
	oo (ehs-PEH-ly-oo) reh-troh-vee-ZOH
seatbelt	*o cinto de segurança*
	oo SEEN-too dee seh-goo-RAHN-sah
steering wheel	*o volante*
	oo voh-LAHN-tee
tire	*o pneu*
	oo pee-NEH-oo
trunk	*o bagageiro; o porta-malas*
	oo bah-gah-ZHEY-roo; oo POHR-tah mah-lahs
windshield	*o pára-brisas*
	oo pah-rah-BREE-zah
windshield wipers	*o limpador de pára-brisas*
	oo LEEN-pah-doh dee pah-rah-BREE-zah

Useful Driving Vocabulary

Here are some essential verbs related to driving. You might hear a taxi driver utter them, or you might want to give them instructions. They may also come in handy if you decide to take a roadtrip during your travels. If you do decide to rent a car in Brazil, make sure you follow the essential rules of the road: know exactly where you are going, have a pre-paid cell phone with you, do not ingest alcohol, and avoid driving during the holidays, when most Brazilians are out on the road.

to pass/overtake	*ultrapassar*
	OO-trah-pah-SAH
to slow down	*diminuir a velocidade*
	dee-mee-noo-EEH ah veh-loh-see-DAH-dee
to yield	*dar a preferência*
	DAH ah preh-feh-REHN-see-ah
to get a ticket	*receber uma multa; ser multado*
	heh-seh-BEH OOHN-a MOO-tah; SEH moo-TAH-doo
to give a ticket	*dar uma multa*
	dah OOHN-ah MOO-tah
to pull over to the side of the road	*parar no acostamento*
	pah-RAH noo ah-KOHS-tah-MEHN-too
to get gas	*pôr gasolina*
	POH gah-zoo-LEEN-nah
to fill it up	*encher o tanque*
	ehn-SHEH roo TAHN-kee
to hitchhike	*pedir carona*
	peh-DEEH kah-ROHN-nah
to park	*estacionar*
	ehs-tah-see-oh-NAH
to turn	*dar a volta*
	dah rah VOHL-tah

to drive	*dirigir, conduzir*
	dee-ree-ZHEE; kohn-doo-ZEEH
to travel	*viajar*
	vee-ah-JAH
to cross	*atravesar*
	ah-trah-veh-SAH
to buckle your seat belt	*apertar o cinto de segurança*
	ah-pehr-TAH oo SEEN-too dee seh-goo-RAHN-sah

 Essential

You might find driving in Brazilian cities to be intimidating. As you attempt to drive around São Paulo or Rio, keep in mind that Brazilians rarely stay in the designated lanes. Always check your rearview mirrors and expect very aggressive drivers. Also watch out for motorcycles: they often go between lanes and do not look for cars or trucks. Don't be surprised to hear more honking and beeping than usual. Most Brazilians do follow the rules of the road, so expect to do the same.

CHAPTER 7

Time for Dinner

Many exotic foods can be enjoyed in Brazil. From fish cooked in coconut sauce to black bean and pork stew, you will find that there are as many different tastes as there are people. The immigrant movement brought exquisite cuisine to Brazil from Italy, Japan, Lebanon, Germany, and many other places. The following sections will help you order the foods you love in Portuguese.

Eating Out

When dining in a restaurant, there are a number of common phrases you will need to know. The following list compiles some of these examples to help you order with ease.

MEALS AND COURSES	
meal	*a refeição*
	ah hey-fey-SAHN-oo
breakfast	*o café da manhã*
	oo kah-FEH dah MANH-nyAHN
lunch	*o almoço*
	oo ahw-MOHL-soo
dinner	*o jantar*
	oo jahn-TAH
snack	*a merenda*
	ah meh-REHN-dah
appetizer	*a entrada*
	ah ehn-TRAH-dah
entrée/main dish	*o prato principal*
	oo PRAH-too preen-see-PAHL
soup	*a sopa*
	ah SOH-pah
salad	*a salada*
	ah sah-LAH-dah
dessert	*a sobremesa*
	ah soh-breh-MEH-zah
wine list	*a carta de vinhos*
	ah KARH-tah dee VEEN-nyoos

MEALS AND COURSES (*CONTINUED*)

menu	o cardápio
	oo kahr-DAH-pee-oo
seafood	*frutos do mar*
	FROO-tohs doo MAH

 Essential

Some restaurants in Brazil serve an appetizer before the main meal called o *couvert*, which can consist of bread, olives, and sometimes quail eggs. But watch out! Even if they bring it to the table without you asking, they will charge for it. It's better to say no if you do not intend to eat it and you are on a budget. On the other hand, you will notice that most main dishes in Brazil serve two or three people. Always ask if it is an individual portion.

BASIC RESTAURANT VOCABULARY

restaurant	*o restaurante*
	oo hehs-tahw-RAHN-tee
buffet-style restaurant	*self-serve/comida a quilo*
	sehl-fee-SEHR-ve/koh-MEE-dah ah KEE-loh
kitchen	*a cozinha*
	ah koo-ZEEN-nee-ah
waiter	*o garçom*
	oo gahr-SOHN
waitress	*a garçonete*
	ah gahr-SOHN-neh-tee
cook	*o chef (de cozinha)*
	oo SHEH-fee (dee koo-ZEEN-nee-ah)

BASIC RESTAURANT VOCABULARY (*CONTINUED*)

pizzeria	*a pizzaria*
	ah pee-tsah-REE-ah
bakery	*a padaria*
	ah pah-dah-REE-ya
bartender	*o barista; o garçom de bar*
	oo bah-REES-tah; oo gahr-SOHN dee bahr
cover (at a club, bar)	*o covert artístico*
	oo koo-VEHR ahr-TEES-tee-koo
valet parking attendant	*o manobrista*
	oo mahn-noh-BREES-tah

Foods

Brazil is a multicultural country, so you will find the world's renowned cuisines well represented and enjoyed by Brazilians, especially in large centers, such as São Paulo and Rio. Don't be afraid to order something you've never had before!

 Alert

In Brazil most steak houses or *churrascarias* (shoo-hahs-kah-REE-ahs) serve beef *ao ponto* (ah-oo POHN-too) or medium. If you would like rare, ask for *mal passado* (mahw-oo pah-SAH-doo) and if you prefer well done, ask for *bem passado* (behn-ee pah-SAH-doo).

TYPES OF MEAT

beef	*carne (de boi)*
	KAHR-nee (dee BOH-yee)
chicken	*frango*
	FRAHN-goo
ham	*presunto*
	preh-ZOOHN-too
lamb	*carneiro*
	kahr-NAY-roo
liver	*fígado*
	FEE-gah-doo
meat	*carne*
	KAHR-nee
pork	*(carne de) porco*
	(KAHR-nee dee) POHR-koo
sausage	*a salsicha*
	ah sah-oo-SEE-shah
seafood	*frutos do mar*
	FROO-toos doo MAH
steak	*bife*
	BEE-fee
turkey	*peru*
	peh-ROO
veal	*(carne de) vitela*
	(KAHR-nee dee) vee-TEH-lah
shrimp	*camarão*
	kah-mah-RANHW-oo
octopus	*polvo*
	POH-oo-voo

 **Essential**

If you are a vegetarian (*vegetariano/a*), it might be challenging to travel in and around Brazil. A large part of the local cuisine is very much centered on red meat, and there are not many choices for vegetarians. However, this is changing slowly, especially in large city centers. Strict vegetarians or vegans are called *veganos*: they follow the *dieta vegana*, which does not include animal products or by-products.

Here are the typical appetizers served in Brazilian restaurants. You might find them in a buffet-style area that you can visit and bring to your table.

COMIDINHAS/APERITIVOS	SNACKS/APPETIZERS
PORTUGUESE	ENGLISH
pastel de queijo pahs-TEH-oo dee KEH-ee-joo	cheese turnover
pastel de carne pahs-TEH-oo dee KAHR-nee	beef turnover
casquinha de siri kahs-KEE-ny-ah dee see-REE	crab meat in shell with bread crumbs and spices
mussarela de búfala moo-sah-REH-lah dee BOO-fah-lah	buffalo mozzarella cheese
coxinha koh-SHEE-ny-ah	chicken stuffed pastry
empada ehn-PAH-dah	shrimp and olive stuffed pastry

PORTUGUESE	ENGLISH
batata frita	French fries
bah-TAH-tah FREE-tah	
azeitonas	olives
ah-zey-TOHN-nahs	
beterrabas	beets
beh-teh-HAH-bahs	
ovo de codorna	quail eggs
OH-voo dee koh-DOHR-nah	

 Essential

Brazilians typically eat the largest meal of the day around noon. Breakfast is usually just a cup of coffee and a baguette or toast with butter. Supper time or dinner consists of a light meal: either some leftovers from lunch, or some soup and bread. Many Brazilians drink coffee in the evening as well.

VEGETABLES AND LEGUMES	
PORTUGUESE	ENGLISH
alface	lettuce
ah-oo-FAH-see	
folhas mixtas	mixed greens
FOH-ly-ahs MEES-tahs	
cebola	onion
seh-BOH-lahs	
cenoura	carrot
seh-NO-rah	

VEGETABLES AND LEGUMES (*CONTINUED*)

PORTUGUESE	ENGLISH
cogumelo koh-goo-MEH-loo	mushroom
feijão fey-JAHN-oo	beans
cebolinho seh-boh-LEEN-oo	green onion
broto de feijão broh-too dee fey-JAHN-oo	sprouts
grão de bico GRAHN-oo dee BEE-koo	chick peas
abacate ah-bah-KAH-tee	avocado
abóbora ah-BOH-boh-rah	squash
abobrinha (italiana) ah-boh-BREEN-nyah	zucchini squash
rúcula HOO-koo-lah	arugula
repolho heh-POH-lyoo	cabbage
pepino peh-PEE-noo	cucumber
gengibre jehn-GEE-bree	ginger

In a typical restaurant menu in São Paulo, you might find a section for *massas* or pastas; you will be able to order *fusilli*, *spaguetti*, *gnocci*, *penne*, *lasagna*, *risotto*, and a variety of Italian dishes. It's also typical for Brazilians to enjoy Japanese cuisine and experiment with *sushi* and *sashimi*. You might find different configurations of sushi rolls that include tropical fruits such as mango, avocado, and pineapple!

Beverages

When you are out and about in cities in Brazil, you will need to know the names of drinks and other beverages. The following is a list of popular Brazilian drinks as well as standard drinks you might be more famililar with from home. Bottoms up!

PORTUGUESE	ENGLISH
água	(tap) water
AH-gwah	
água filtrada	filtered water
AH-gwah feel-TRAH-dah	
água mineral (sem gás)	mineral water (not carbonated)
AH-gwah mee-neh-RAHL (sehn GAHS)	
água mineral com gás	seltzer water
AH-gwah mee-neh-RAHL kohn GAHS	(carbonated water)
refrigerante	soft drink
heh-free-geh-RAHN-tee	
coca-cola	Coca-Cola
KOH-kah KOH-lah	
guaraná	Brazilian soft drink made from
gwah-rah-NAH	guaraná plant

PORTUGUESE	ENGLISH
suco de laranja SOO-koo dee lah-RAHN-jah	orange juice
suco de limão SOO-koo dee lee-MAHN-oo	lime (or lemon) juice
limonada suíça lee-moh-NAH-dah soo-EE-sah	lime juice blended with ice and water
leite LAY-tee	milk
chá gelado SHAH geh-LAH-doo	iced tea

ALCOHOLIC BEVERAGES

PORTUGUESE	ENGLISH
vodca VOH-dee-kah	vodka
gin GEEN	gin
uísque oo-EES-kee	whiskey
vinho branco VEEN-nyoo BRAHN-koo	white wine
vinho tinto VEEN-nyoo TEEN-too	red wine
vinho rosé VEEN-nyoo ho-ZEH	blush wine
cachaça kah-SHAH-sah	Brazilian rum
rum HOON	rum

Dishes and Silverware

During your travels around Brazil, you may find yourself in need of some silverware or dishes. If you need to ask for another fork or napkin, here's the vocabulary you'll need to do so easily.

ENGLISH	PORTUGUESE
bowl	*tijela*; *prato de sopa*
	tee-JEH-lah; PRAH-too dee SOH-pah
cup	*xícara*
	SHEE-kah-rah
fork	*garfo*
	GAHR-foo
glass	*copo*
	KOH-poo
wine glass	*taça*
	TAH-sah
knife	*faca*
	FAH-kah
napkin	*guardanapo*
	gwahr-dahn-NAH-poo
plate	*prato*
	PRAH-too
silverware	*talheres*
	tahl-YEA-rees
spoon	*colher de sopa*
	kohl-YEA dee SOH-pah
teaspoon	*colher de chá*
	kohl-YEA dee SHAH

Ordering Your Meal

Some expressions in Portuguese are essential when ordering your meal or talking about food. The following are some of the most common words and phrases you will need to know.

ENGLISH	PORTUGUESE
to be hungry	*ter fome*
	tehr FOHN-mee
to be thirsty	*ter sede*
	tehr SEH-dee
to order	*pedir*
	peh-DEER
to drink	*beber*
	beh-BEHR
to eat	*comer*
	koh-MEHR
check/bill	*a conta*
	ah KOHN-tah
cover charge	*couvert*
	koo-VEHR
menu	*cardápio*
	kahr-DAH-pee-oo
tip	*gorgeta*
	gohr-JEH-tah

Dietary Restrictions

Sometimes you need to communicate about the items that you cannot consume, rather than what you do want or can eat. Here are some expressions that you might need to use in Brazilian restaurants.

ENGLISH	PORTUGUESE
I'm vegetarian.	*Sou vegetariano/a.*
	soo veh-geh-tah-ree-AHN-noo/-ah
I'm a vegan.	*Sou vegano/a.*
	soo veh-GAHN-noo/-ah
I'm on a diet.	*Estou de dieta.*
	ehs-toow dee dee-EH-tah
I'm allergic.	*Sou alérgico/a.*
	soo ah-LEHR-gee-koo/-ah
I'm a diebetic.	*Sou diabético/a.*
	soo dee-ah-BEH-tee-koo/-ah
It's too salty.	*Está muito salgado.*
	ehs-TAH moohn-yee-too sahl-GAH-doo
I would rather have it	*Prefiro com pouca pimenta.*
less spicy.	preh-FEE-roo kohn POHoo-kah pee-MEHN-tah
I don't drink.	*Eu não bebo.*
	eh-oo nahn-oo BEH-boo

CHAPTER 8

Shopping and Services

During your travels, you may find you want to make a few purchases to remember your trip to Brazil. The following sections will introduce you to the places you can spend money and help you with questions you might want to ask about your purchases. With the right words and some *Reais* or a credit card in hand, you will be ready to purchase a variety of beautiful items, from clothing to jewelry to artisanal products.

Stores and Businesses

There are many places that will gladly accept your money in exchange for goods and services. Whether you are in the mood for a cup of coffee or would like a new pair of gold earrings, the following list will help you prepare for your purchase. Here is a list of the shopping places that may interest you most:

bakery	*a padaria*
	ah pah-dah-REE-ah
butcher shop	*o açougue*
	oo ah-SOO-ghee
department store	*a loja de departamento*
	ah LOH-jah dee deh-pahr-tah-MEHN-too
dry-cleaner	*lavagem a seco*
	lah-VAH-zhehn ah SEH-koo
fish market	*a peixaria*
	ah pay-shah-REE-ah
grocery store/supermarket	*o supermercado*
	oo soo-pehr-mehr-CAH-doo
jewelry shop	*a joalheria*
	ah joh-ah-LYEH-ree-ah
newsstand	*a banca de revista*
	ah BAHN-kah dee reh-VEES-tah
outdoor market	*a feira*
	ah FEY-rah
pastry shop	*a pastelaria*
	ah pahs-teh-lah-REE-ah

pharmacy	*a farmácia*
	ah fahr-MAH-see-ah
store	*a loja*
	ah LOH-jah

 **Essential**

While it is true that in the past, Brazilians used to shop at the bakery, butcher's shop, and the fishmonger's separately, nowadays most people simply go to the grocery store and buy everything they need, much like in the United States. That said, there are many street markets where you can buy fresh fruit, called *feiras*, and they are comparatively cheaper.

Laundromat and Dry-Cleaner

Did you spill some wine on the only dress shirt you brought with you? Perhaps there is an oil stain on your blouse? If you are in a four-star hotel, you can have laundry services take care of the problem. If not, there are dry-cleaning services in Brazil, but laundromats are not easily found. Here are some words that will help you with the task of getting your clothes clean and spotless.

to wash	*lavar*
	lah-VAH
to dry-clean	*lavar a seco*
	lah-VAH ah SEH-koo

to dry	*enxugar*
	ehn-shoo-GAH
bleach	*água sanitária*
	AH-gwa sahn-nee-TAH-ree-ah
dryer	*a secadora*
	ah seh-kah-DOH-rah
fabric softener	*o amaciante*
	oo ah-mah-see-AHN-tee
to do the laundry	*lavar a roupa*
	lah-VAH ah HO-pah
soap (in powdered form)	*o sabão (em pó)*
	oo sah-BAHN-oo (ehn-ee POH)
stain	*a mancha*
	ah MAHN-shah
starch(ed)	*engomado*
	ehn-gohn-MAH-doo
washing machine	*a lavadora*
	ah lah-vah-DOH-rah

 **Essential**

It is probably true that if you are a guest to a Brazilian middle class family, they will have a maid that will wash, iron, and fold your clothes for you. Make sure to give her a monetary reward for her services before you leave. If you are at a very nice hotel, they will also have laundry services that you might use. Coin-operated laundromats do not exist in Brazil.

Hair Salon and Barbershop

Brazilian hairstylists are among the best in the world. You'll find that prices can be reasonable, especially in a barbershop. Hey, you're on vacation—give it a try! Also, Brazilians are excellent in nail and skin care. If you are on vacation, make sure to get a manicure/pedicure at a reputable beauty salon.

barber	*o barbeiro*
	oo bahr-BAY-roo
hair salon	*o salão de beleza*
	oo sah-LAHN-oo dee beh-LEH-zah
beard	*a barba*
	ah BAHR-bah
beauty parlor	*o cabelereiro*
	oo kah-bay-leh-REY-roo
brush	*a escova*
	ah ehs-KO-vah
comb	*o pente*
	oo PEHN-tee
curls	*os cachos*
	oos KAH-shoos
dandruff	*caspa*
	KAHS-pah
dry hair	*cabelos secos*
	kah-BEH-loos SEH-koos
hair	*o cabelo*
	oo kah-BEH-loo

a haircut	*um corte (de cabelo)*
	oohn KOHR-tee (dee kah-BEH-loo)
hairstyle	*o penteado*
	oo pehn-teh-AH-doo
hairstylist	*o cabelereiro*
	oo kah-beh-ley-REY-roo
long	*longo*
	LOHN-goo
moustache	*bigode*
	bee-GOH-dee
oily hair	*cabelo oleoso*
	kah-BEH-loo oh-leh-OH-zoo
part	*onde você parte*
	ohn-dee voh-SAY PAHR-tee
short	*curto*
	KOOHR-too
bangs	*franja*
	FRAHN-jah
a trim	*uma aparada*
	oohn-ah ah-pah-RAH-dah
wig	*uma perruca*
	oonh-ah peh-ROO-kah

VERBS

to blow dry	*secar*
	seh-KAH
to curl	*encaracolar*
	ehn-kah-rah-koh-LAH
to cut	*cortar*
	kohr-TAH

VERBS (CONTINUED)

to perm	*fazer um permanente*
	fah-ZEH oohn pehr-mahn-NEHN-tee
to shave	*fazer a barba*
	fah-ZEH rah BAHR-bah
to wash	*lavar*
	lah-VAH
to do someone's hair	*fazer o cabelo*
	fah-ZEH roo cah-BEH-loo
to dye; to color	*tingir*
	teen-JIHR
to brush	*escovar*
	ehs-koo-VAH
to comb	*pentear*
	pehn-teh-AH

Clothing and Jewelry

You can find a lot of fashion in Brazilian cities. While sometimes it is fun just to browse, you may find yourself in need of a new shirt or pants while traveling. It's important to know the names of the specific types of clothing that you might need to purchase while traveling.

CLOTHING

bathing suit (for women)	*o maiô*
	oo mah-ee-OH
bathing suit (for men)	*o calção (de banho)*
	oo kahl-SAHN-oo (dee BAHN-nyoo)

CLOTHING (CONTINUED)

belt	*o cinto*
	oo SEEN-too
blouse	*a blusa*
	ah BLOO-sah
boots	*as botas*
	ahs BOH-tahs
bra	*o sutiã*
	oo soo-tee-AHN
clothes	*a roupa*
	ah HO-pah
dress	*o vestido*
	oo vehs-TEE-doo
footwear	*o calçado*
	oo kahl-SAH-doo
glasses	*os óculos*
	oo ZOH-koo-lohs
gloves	*as luvas*
	ahs LOO-vahs
hat	*o chapéu*
	oo shah-PEH-oo
jacket	*a jaqueta*
	ah jah-KEH-tah
jeans	*os jeans*
	oohs JEENS
lining	*o forro*
	oo FOH-hoo
makeup	*a maquiagem*
	ah mah-kee-AH-zhehn

CLOTHING (CONTINUED)

overcoat	*o casaco*
	oo kah-SAH-koo
pajamas	*o pijama*
	oo pee-JAHN-mah
panties	*a calcinha*
	ah kahl-SEEN-nya
pants	*as calças*
	ahs KAHL-sahs
perfume	*o perfume*
	oo pehr-FOO-mee
raincoat	*o casaco de chuva*
	oo kah-ZAH-koo dee SHOO-vah
sandals	*as sandálias*
	ahs sahn-DAH-lee-ahs
scarf	*o lenço*; *o cachecol* (for winter)
	oo LEHN-soo; oo kah-shee-KOHL
shirt	*a camisa*
	ah kah-MEE-zah
shoes	*os sapatos*
	oohs sah-PAH-toos
skirt	*a saia*
	ah SAH-ee-ya
sneakers	*o (sapato) tênis*
	oo (sah-PAH-too) TEHN-nees
socks	*as meias*
	ahs MAY-yee-ahs
stocking	*a meia-calça*
	ah MAY-yee-ah-KAHL-sah

CLOTHING (CONTINUED)

suit	*o terno*
	oo TEHR-noo
sunglasses	*os óculos escuros; os óculos de sol*
	ooh ZOH-koo-loos zehs-KOO-roos;
	ooh ZOH-koo-loos dee SOHL
sweater	*a suéter*
	ah soo-EH-tehr
tie	*a gravata*
	ah grah-VAH-tah
T-shirt	*a camiseta*
	ah kah-mee-ZEH-tah
underwear	*a roupa íntima*
	ah HO-pah EEN-tee-mah

MISCELLANEOUS

zipper	*o flechecler*
	oo fleh-sheh-KLEH
wallet	*a carteira*
	ah karh-TEY-rah
spike heel	*o salto alto*
	oo SAHL-too AHL-too
sleeve	*a manga*
	ah MAHN-gah
shoelace	*o cardaço*
	oo kahr-DAH-soo
pocket	*o bolso*
	oo BOHL-soo
lipstick	*o batom*
	oo bah-TOHN

MISCELLANEOUS (*CONTINUED*)

handbag	*a bolsa*
	ah BOHL-sah
umbrella	*a sombrinha* (women)
	o guarda-chuva (men)
	ah sohn-BREEN-ny-ah/oo gwahr-dah SHOO-vah
button	*o botão*
	oo boh-TAHN-oo
cloth; fabric; material	*o tecido*
	oo teh-SEE-doh
color	*a cor*
	ah KOHR

MATERIALS

cotton	*algodão*
	ah-goo-DAHN-oo
wool	*a lã*
	ah LAHN
velvet	*o veludo*
	oo veh-LOO-doo
silk	*a seda*
	ah SEH-dah
leather	*o couro*
	oo KO-roo

USEFUL VERBS

to button up	*abotoar*
	ah-boh-toh-AH
to change; to get changed	*mudar (de roupa)*
	moo-DAH (dee HO-pah)
to dress (oneself);	*vestir-se*
to get dressed	vehs-TEER-see
to fit; to suit	*ficar bem*
	fee-KAH behn
to knot; to tie	*dar um nó*
	dah roohn NOH
to measure	*medir*
	meh-DEEh
to mend; to repair; to darn	*remendar*
	heh-mehn-DAH
to sew	*costurar*
	kohs-too-RAH
to take off; to remove	*tirar, remover*
	tee-RAH; reh-mo-VEH
to try	*provar*
	proh-VAH
to unbutton; to undo	*desabotoar*
	deh-zah-boh-toh-AH
to undress (oneself);	*tirar (a roupa); despir-se*
to get undressed	tee-RAH (ah HO-pah); dehs-PEEH-see

Jewelry and Stones

Brazil is known for its great geological richness. If you are a fan of beautiful semi-precious stones, you are in for a treat. There is fantastic artistry among jewelry makers in Brazil. Why not bring something beautiful home with you from South America? Here are some words that you might need in order to make that special purchase.

JEWELRY	
amber	*âmbar*
	AHN-bahr
bracelet	*a pulseira*
	ah pool-SAY-rah
brooch	*o broche*
	oo BROH-shee
costume jewelry	*a bijouteria*
	ah bee-joo-teh-REE-ah
cufflinks	*as abotoaduras*
	ahs zah-boh-too-ah-DOO-rahs
diamond	*o diamante*
	oo dee-ah-MAHN-tee
earrings	*os brincos*
	oos BREEN-koos
emerald	*a esmeralda*
	ah ehs-meh-RAHL-dah
gold	*o ouro*
	oo OH-roo
gold plated	*dourado*
	do-RAH-doo

JEWELRY (CONTINUED)

jewelry	*as jóias*
	ahs JOY-yas
necklace	*o colar*
	oo koh-LAH
pearls	*as pérolas*
	ahs PEH-roh-lahs
pendant	*o pinjente*
	oo peen-JEHN-tee
pin	*o broche*
	oo BROH-shee
ring	*o anel*
	oo AHN-neh-oo
ruby	*o rubi*
	oo hoo-BEE
sapphire	*a safira*
	ah sah-FEE-rah
silver	*a prata*
	ah PRAH-tah
silver plated	*prateado*
	prah-teh-AH-doo
watch	*o relógio*
	ooh eh-LOH-zhee-oo
wedding ring	*a aliança*
	ah ah-lee-AHN-sah

Useful Adjectives:
Color, Texture, and More

The following list may come in handy when you are out and about shopping in Brazil. Remember that, in Portuguese, colors are adjectives and therefore they must agree in number and gender with the nouns they modify.

attractive	*atraente*
	ah-trah-EHN-tee
black	*preto*
	PREH-too
dark blue	*azul*
	ah-ZOOL
brown	*marrom*
	mah-HOHN
comfortable	*confortável; cómodo*
	kohn-fohr-TAH-veh-oo; KOH-moh-doh
elegant	*elegante*
	eh-leh-GAHN-tee
fashionable; in fashion	*na moda*
	nah MOH-da
gold (in color); golden	*dourado*
	doh-RAH-doo
(made) of gold; gold	*de ouro*
	dee OH-roo
gray	*cinza; cinzento*
	SEEN-zha; seehn-zehn-too
green	*verde*
	VEHR-dee

long	*longo*
	LOHN-goo
naked; nude	*nu*
	noo
orange	*laranja*
	lah-RAHN-jah
pink	*rosa*
	HOH-zah
purple	*roxo*
	HO-shoo
violet	*violeta; lilás*
	vee-oh-LEH-tah; lee-LAHS
red	*vermelho*
	vehr-MEH-lyoo
short	*curto*
	KOOR-too
silver (in color); silvery	*prateado*
	prah-teh-AH-doo
(made) of silver; silver	*de prata*
	dee PRAH-tah
soft; smooth	*liso*
	lee-ZOO
rough	*áspero*
	AHS-peh-roo
thick	*espesso*
	ehs-PEH-soo
tight (fitting)	*apertado*
	ah-pehr-TAH-doo
white	*branco*
	BRAHN-koo

worn out	*desgastado*
	dehs-gahs-TAH-doo
yellow	*amarelo*
	ah-mah-REH-loo

Useful Adjectives: Sizes

Shoe and clothing sizes in Brazil are different than those used in the United States. Be prepared for the shoe salesman to tell you that you have a size 39 foot, which is equivalent to a size 9½ in the United States. Make sure to ask the clerk at the shoe store to measure your shoe size. Shoe stores in Brazil have excellent customer service.

What size do you wear?
Qual o tamanho que o senhor/a senhora usa?
kwa oo tah-MAHN-nyoo keh oo sehn-NY-oh/ah sehn-NYO-rah oo-zah

I would like . . .
Gostaria de . . .
gohs-tah-REE-aah dee

I don't know the sizes here in Brazil.
Eu não conheço os tamanhos aqui no Brasil.
EH-oo NHAN-oo kohn-NYE-soo oosh tah-MAHN-nyoos zah-kee noo brah-ZEE-oo

It's too big/small.

É muito grande/pequeno.

EH MOO-yin-too GRAHN-dee/peh-KEH-no

CLOTHING SIZE (*LA TAGLIA/LA MISURA*)	
large	*grande*
	GRAHN-dee
larger	*maior*
	MAH-ye-OH
medium	*médio*
	MEH-dee-oo
small	*pequeno*
	peh-KEH-noo
smaller	*menor*
	meh-NOH

CHAPTER 9

Brazilian Portuguese for Business

Though you will find that many Brazilians are somewhat proficient in English, you will certainly gain the respect of your Brazilian colleagues by demonstrating a proficiency in their language. If you're traveling to São Paulo or Brasília for business, the following will help you make a good impression on your Brazilian Portuguese-speaking colleagues!

Jobs and Professions

Knowing how to refer to a wide variety of professions and jobs can only enhance your business interactions. The following list names many professions, including the masculine and feminine forms of each one (as indicated by the appropriate article and/or ending). Sometimes the same word is used for both, except that the definite article changes (*o* for males and *a* for females).

accountant	*o/a contabilista*
	oo/ah kohn-tah-bee-LEES-tah
apprentice	*o/a aprendiz*
	oo/ah ah-prehn-DEES
banker	*o banqueiro* (usually a male)
	oo bahn-kehy-roo
bank teller	*o bancário/a bancária*
	oo bahn-KAH-ree-oo/ah bahn-KAH-ree-ah
biologist	*o biólogo/a bióloga*
	oo bee-OH-loh-goo/ah bee-OH-loh-gah
broker	*o corrector/a correctora*
	oo koh-heh-TOHR/ah koh-heh-TOH-rah
cashier	*o/a caixa*
	oo/ah KAH-ee-shah
civil servant	*o funcionário público/a funcionária pública*
	oo foohn-see-oo-NAH-ree-oo POO-blee-koo/
	ah foohn-see-oo-NAH-ree-ah POO-blee-kah
dentist	*o/a dentista*
	oo/ah dehn-TEES-tah

detective	*o/a detetive*
	oo/ah deh-teh-TEE-veh
doctor	*o doutor/a doutora*
	oo doh-TOH/ah doh-TOH-rah
economist	*o/a economista*
	oo/ah eh-koh-noh-MEES-tah
employee	*o empregado/a empregada*
	oo ehn-preh-GAH-doo/ah ehn-preh-GAH-dah
engineer	*o engenheiro/a engenheira*
	oo ehn-zhehn-ny-EH-roo/ah ehn-zhehn-ny-EH-rah
judge	*o juiz/a juíza*
	oo joo-EES/ah joo-EE-zah
journalist	*o/a jornalista*
	oo/ah johr-nah-LEES-tah
lawyer	*o advogado/a advogada*
	oo ah-dee-voh-GAH-doh/ah ah-dee-voh-GAH-dah
manager	*o/a gerente*
	oo/ah geh-REHN-tee
notary	*o notário/a notária*
	oo noh-TAH-ree-oo/ah noh-TAH-ree-ah
nurse	*o enfermeiro/a enfermeira*
	oo ehn-fehr-MEY-roo/ah ehn-fehr-MEY-rah
pharmacist	*o farmacêutico/a farmacêutica*
	oo fahr-mah-SEH-oo-tee-koo/ah fahr-mah-SEH-oo-tee-kah
pilot	*o/a piloto*
	oo/ah pee-LOH-too
police officer	*o/a policial*
	oo/ah poh-lee-see-AL
president	*o/a presidente*
	oo/ah preh-zee-DEHN-tee

receptionist	*o/a recepcionista*
	oo/ah heh-sep-see-ohn-NEES-tah
researcher	*o pesquisador/a pesquisadora*
	oo pehs-kee-zah-DOHR/ah pehs-kee-zah-DOH-rah
scientist	*o/a cientista*
	oo/ah see-ehn-TEES-tah
secretary	*a secretária* (usually female)
	ah seh-kreh-TAH-ree-ah
soldier	*o/a soldado*
	oo/ah sohl-DAH-doo
stockbroker	*o corretor/a corretora de ações*
	oo koh-heh-TOHR/ah koh-heh-TOHR-ah dee ah-SOHN-ees
technician	*o técnico/a técnica*
	oo TEHK-nee-koh/ah TEHK-nee-kah
writer	*o escritor/a escritora*
	oo ehs-kree-TOHR/ah ehs-kree-TOH-rah

 Fact

Brazilian business offices are open on Mondays through Fridays from 8:00 A.M. to 12:00 P.M. and again from 1:00–4:00 P.M. Banks are open during those times as well, except without the lunch break. Bank workers usually have morning and afternoon shifts. Stores are open Mondays to Saturdays from 9:00 A.M. until closing time, usually around 9:00 P.M.

Brazilian Portuguese on the Job

Here is an introduction to vocabulary related to white-collar professions.

boss; manager	*o gerente* (usually male)
	oo geh-REHN-tee
business card	*o cartão de visita*
	oo kahr-TAHN-oo dee vee-ZEE-tah
CEO	*o chefe da empresa* (usually male)
	oo SHEH-fee dah ehn-PREH-zah
company	*a companhia*; *a empresa*
	ah kohn-pahn-NEE-ah; ah ehn-PREH-zah
contract	*o contrato*
	oo kohn-TRAH-too
corporate planning	*o planejamento empresarial*
	oo plah-neh-jah-MEHN-too ehn-preh-zah-ree-AH-oo
interview	*a entrevista*
	ah ehn-treh-VEES-tah
job	*o emprego*
	oo ehn-PREH-goo
meeting	*a reunião*
	ah heh-oo-nee-AHN-oo
raise	*o aumento salarial*
	oo ah-oo-MEHN-too sah-lah-ree-AHL
resumé	*o currículo (vitae)*
	oo koo-HEE-koo-loo (VEE-teh)
salary	*o salário*
	oo sah-LAH-ree-oo

unemployed	*desempregado/a*
	deh-zehn-preh-GAH-doo/-dah
unemployment	*o desemprego*
	oo deh-zehn-PREH-goo
to hire	*empregar*
	ehn-prehn-GAH
to fire	*despedir*
	dehs-peh-DEER
to work	*trabalhar*
	trah-bah-LY-AH

 Alert

Brazilian workers usually receive their paychecks on a monthly basis. In December, they normally receive an end-of-year bonus, called *o décimo terceiro* (oo DEH-see-moo tehr-SAY-roo; the thirteenth, as in the thirteenth paycheck of the year), which is equivalent to one month's salary.

On the Phone

One must use a more formal greeting when conducting business over the phone. To start, you'll need to know that when Brazilians pick up the phone, they might say *Pois não?* (pronounced "poh-yees-NAHN-oo") or a more formal name of the company.

Hello, may I speak to . . . ?
Alô, posso falar com . . . ?
ah-LOH, POH-soo fah-LAH kohn . . .

Good morning, I would like to speak to . . .
Bom dia, gostaria de falar com . . .
bohn DEE-ah, gohs-tah-REE-ah dee fah-LAH kohn . . .

Who is calling?
Quem fala?
kehn-yee FAH-lah

Please hold.
Aguarde, por favor.
ah-GWAH-dee pohr fah-VOH

I'll put you through now.
Vou transferir agora.
voh-oo trahns-feh-REE ah-GOH-rah

I'm sorry, he's not here. Would you like to leave a message?
Sinto muito, mas ele não está. A senhora gostaria de deixar uma mensagem?
SEEN-too moo-yeen-too, mahs EH-lee NAHN-oo ehs-TAH. Ah senh-NYO-rah gohs-tah-REE-ah dee dey-SHAH uhn-ah mehn-SAH-jehn

TERMS FOR PHONE USAGE

answering machine	*a secretária eletrônica*
	ah seh-kreh-TAH-ree-ah eh-leh-TROH-nee-kah
phonebook	*a agenda telefônica*
	ah ah-ZHEHN-dah teh-leh-FOHN-nee-kah
phone number	*o número de telefone*
	oo NOO-meh-roo dee teh-leh-FOHN-nee
to call	*chamar, telefonar*
	shah-MAH; teh-leh-fohn-NAH
to call back	*retornar*
	heh-tohr-NAH
to dial the number	*discar o número*
	dees-KAH oo NOO-meh-roo
to hang up	*desligar*
	dehs-lee-GAH
to leave a message	*deixar uma mensagem*
	deh-ye-SHAH oonh-aa mehn-SAH-zhehn
to ring	*estar tocando*
	ehs-TAH toh-KAHN-doo

 **Essential**

When making a phone call in Brazil, try to be as polite as possible, especially if you don't know the person who is answering the phone. You should use the terms *boa tarde* (good afternoon), *por favor* (please), and *obrigado/a* (thank you) whenever possible.

Office Supplies and Equipment

This section is designed to aid you in getting all the supplies you need in an office. You never know when you will need the word "stapler" in Portuguese!

blotter	*mata-borrão*
	MAH-tah boh-HUHN-oo
cabinet	*o armário*
	oo ahr-MAH-ree-oo
clerical assistant	*o/a assistente*
	oo/ah ah-sees-TEHN-tee
clock	*o relógio*
	oo heh-LOH-zhee-oo
desk	*a escrivaninha; a mesa*
	ah ehs-kree-vahn-nee-nya; ah MEH-zah
desk drawer	*a gaveta*
	ah gah-VEH-tah
felt-tip pen	*a caneta hidrográfica*
	ah kah-NEH-tah ee-droh-GRAH-fee-kah
filing cabinet	*o armário-arquivo; o fichário*
	oo ahr-MAH-ree-oo-ahr-kee-voo;
	oo fee-SHAH-ree-oo
keyboard	*o teclado*
	oo teh-KLAH-doo
paperclip	*o clipe (de papel)*
	oo KLEE-pee (dee pah-PEHL)
partition wall	*a parede divisória*
	ah pah-REH-dee dee-vee-SOH-ree-ah

pen	*a caneta*
	ah kah-NEH-tah
pencil sharpener	*o apontador de lápis*
	oo ah-pohn-tah-DOH dee LAH-pees
pocket calculator	*a calculadora*
	ah kahl-koo-lah-DOH-rah
printer	*a impressora*
	ah een-preh-SOH-rah
hole puncher	*o perfurador*
	oo pehr-foo-rah-DOH
ruler	*a regla*
	ah HEH-glah
scanner	*o escaner*
	oo ehs-KAHN-neh
stapler	*o grampeador*
	oo grahn-peh-ah-DOH
suspension file	*o arquivo suspensão*
	oh ahr-KEE-voo soos-pehn-SAHN-oo
wall calendar	*o calendário de parede*
	oo kah-lehn-DAH-ree-oo dee pah-REH-dee
wastepaper basket	*o cesto (de papéis)*
	oo SEHS-too (dee pah-PEH-ees)

Banks and Changing Money

Sometimes tourists will buy traveler's checks before traveling to another country in order to avoid exchanging currency. However, not every local business will accept your traveler's checks. The following section will shed some light on more convenient and perhaps easier ways to get Brazilian currency (*Reais*) while you vacation.

 Fact

> Because famous historical figures would adorn Brazilian bills, and these bills would lose their value so quickly, what was meant to be an honor became a source of ridicule. In later editions of Brazilian currency, images of beautiful species of flowers and native animals have been used.

ATMs Are Called *Banco24Horas*

Buying *Reais* from your bank in the United States can be expensive and sometimes even impossible. Most banks will charge a lot in fees. The same goes for exchanging money at airports, exchange counters, and hotels in Brazil. The best exchange rates can be found at ATMs (*Banco24Horas*, pronounced BAHN-koh-VEEN-tee-KWA-troo-OH-rahs). Check with your bank before you leave to determine if there are any service charges involved with ATM use abroad. Your bank may allow free ATM use through a specific Brazilian network (Cirrus is one of the most widely available). ATMs in Brazil will usually only allow you to withdraw money from your primary account (usually your checking account). If you're used to keeping a low balance in your checking account and a high balance in savings, you may want to call your bank to make sure that your checking and savings accounts are linked. You should also inform your bank of your travel plans. Sometimes your debit card will be blocked from being used overseas due to security measures. You will want to let them know that your card services should be up and running.

Banks

If you do not have an ATM card, your best bet is to exchange money at a bank. Be advised: paperwork can take some time, and, though it may be better than what you find at the airport, the exchange rate might still be high.

Credit Cards

Major credit card accounts usually offer cash advance services. Credit card users can benefit from the antifraud protection that accompanies their accounts (save your receipts!). Although the exchange rates can be comparable, check the types of fees and charges associated with credit card transactions.

Traveler's Checks

Many travelers still insist on the convenience and safety of traveler's checks. Unfortunately, with the prevalence of ATMs and credit card use, travelers will find that traveler's checks are not as widely accepted as they used to be. You might be able to exchange them in banks and in hotels, but don't count on them being accepted at local shops or restaurants.

Useful Vocabulary and Phrases

The following terms and expressions will help you navigate Brazilian financial institutions—or at least they will help you as you try to exchange money.

MONEY AND THE BANK	
money	*o dinheiro*
	ooh DEEN-nyeh-roo
the Real (Brazilian currency)	*Real*; *Reais* (sing.; plural)
	heh-OW; heh-AHYSS
change	*o troco*
	ooh troh-koo
banknote	*a cédula*
	ah SEH-doo-lah
coin	*a moeda*
	ah moo-EH-dah
dollar	*o dólar*
	ooh DOHL-lah
check	*o cheque*
	ooh SHEH-kee
traveler's check	*o travelers cheque*
	ooh trah-veh-lehrs sheh-kee
to cash a check	*descontar um cheque*
	dehs-KOHN-tahr oohn SHEH-kee
bank	*o banco*
	ooh BAHN-koo
counter	*o balcão*
	ooh bow-KAHN-oo
teller window	*o caixa*
	ooh KAH-EE-shah

MONEY AND THE BANK (*CONTINUED*)

exchange rate	*a taxa de cambio*
	ah TAH-shah dee KAHN-bee-oo
to sign	*assinar*
	ah-see-nahr

At the Bank

It will be extremely helpful to know words that relate to the banking industry in Brazil. You will notice that banks are very busy in comparison to the United States, and that they are usually very large. There are very few smaller banks, such as credit unions.

Which is the counter to exchange money?
Qual é o balcão para trocar dinheiro?
KWOO-ahl EH oo bahl-KAHN-oo pah-ra troh-KAH deen-nyeh-roo

Is there a fee (commission)?
Tem uma taxa?
TEHN-ee OONH-a TAH-shah

What's the exchange rate for the dollar?
Qual é a taxa do dólar?
kwahl eh ah TAH-shah doo DOHL-lah

Where do I have to sign?
Onde eu assino?
OHN-dee EH-ew AH-see-noo

What is today's date?
Qual é a data de hoje?
kwahl eh ah DAH-tah dee oh-jee

What time does the bank open?
A que hora abre o banco?
ah keh oh-rah AH-breh oo BAHN-koo

What time does the bank close?
A que hora fecha o banco?
ah keh oh-rah FEH-shah oo BAHN-koo

Do you accept credit cards?
Vocês aceitam cartão de crédito?
Voh-say-ees ah-SAY-tahn KAHR-tahn-oo dee
KREH-dee-too

Can you change money for me?
Vocês podem trocar dinheiro pra mim?
Voh-say-ees poh-DEHN troh-KAH deen-nyehn-roo PAH-
rah meen

Can you change dollars for me?
Vocês podem trocar dólar pra mim?
Voh-say-ees poh-DEHN troh-KAH DOHL-lah PAH-rah meen

Where can I get large notes changed?
Onde posso trocar cédulas grandes?
OHN-dee POH-ssoo troh-KAH SEH-duh-lahs
GRAHN-dees

Where can I get foreign money changed?
Onde posso trocar dinheiro estrangeiro?
OHN-dee POH-ssoo troh-KAH deen-nyehn-roo
ehs-trahn-JEY-roo

Where can I change a traveler's check?
Onde posso trocar travelers cheques?
OHN-dee POH-ssoo troh-KAH trah-veh-lehrs sheh-kee

What is today's exchange rate?
Qual é a taxa de cambio hoje?
KWOO-ahl eh ah TAH-shah dee KAHN-bee-oo OH-jee

Where is an automatic teller machine (ATM)?
Onde tem um banco 24 horas?
OHN-dee TEHN oohn BAHN-koh VEEN-tee-KWA-troo
OH-rahs

 Alert

It is very common for Brazilian banks to go on strike.
The bank workers union is very active and employees
often earn very low wages. If you travel to Brazil, you
might experience closed banks for several days. Make
sure to have your valid credit card with you and you
will be able to continue to make purchases and use the
ATMs around town.

CHAPTER 10

Brazilian Portuguese Medical Phrases

No one wants to think about getting sick while on vacation. Though the hope is that your trip will proceed without a hitch, it's possible that you may need to seek a doctor's advice while you're abroad. The followng sections will give you the words and phrases you might need to know to tell a doctor what's wrong.

Common Ailments and Maladies

Being sick is bad enough, but not being able to communicate what's wrong to a medical professional is even worse. This section gives a list of common ailments that can help you to get the help you need. You can use the verb *ter* (to have) with these medical problems.

allergy	*alergia*
	ah-lehr-JEE-ah
appendicitis	*apendicite*
	ah-pehn-dee-SEE-tee
arthritis	*artrite*
	ahr-TREE-tee
blood poisoning	*septicemia*
	sehp-tee-seh-MEE-ah
chicken pox	*catapora*
	kah-tah-POH-rah
cold	*resfriado*
	hehs-free-AH-doo
cough	*tosse*
	TOH-see
diabetes	*diabete*
	dee-ah-BEH-tee
dizziness	*tontura*
	tohn-TOO-rah
fever	*febre*
	FEH-bree
heatstroke	*insolação*
	een-soh-lah-SAHN-oo

heartburn	*azia*
	ah-ZEE-ah
hypertension	*hipertensão* (or *pressão alta*)
	ee-pehr-tehn-SAHN-oo (preh-SAHN-oo AHL-tah)
insomnia	*insônia*
	een-SOHN-nee-ah
pain	*dor*
	dohr
pneumonia	*pneunonia*
	pee-neh-oo-moh-NEE-ah
sea sickness	*enjôo*
	ehn-JOH-oo
seasick	*mareado*
	mah-reh-AH-doo
sore throat	*garganta inflamada*
	gahr-GAHN-tah een-flah-MAH-dah
sprain	*distensão*
	dees-tehn-SAHN-oo
ulcer	*úlcera*
	UHL-seh-rah
wound	*ferida*
	feh-REE-dah

 Alert

Before you travel to Brazil, make sure to get all your vaccinations checked and updated, so that you are protected from common tropical maladies. Your primary care doctor can let you know if you need special shots.

Another group of illnesses goes with *ser* (to be); for example, "to be (a) diabetic" is *ser diabético*.

asthmatic	*asmático/a*
	ahz-MAH-tee-koh/-ah
diabetic	*diabético/a*
	dee-ah-BEH-tee-koh/-ah
(suffers from) heart condition	*cardíaco/a*
	kahr-DEE-ah-koo/-ah

Here are some useful terms for describing your illness:

I need to take medicine	*preciso tomar remédio*
	preh-SEE-zoo toh-MAH heh-MEH-dee-oo
I have high blood pressure	*tenho pressão alta*; *sou hipertenso*
	TEHN-oo preh-SAHN-oo AHL-tah;
	soo ee-pehr-TEHN-soo
I broke my leg	*quebrei a perna*
	keh-BRAY ah PEHR-na

🔔 Alert

When talking about parts of the body, Portuguese speakers will not say "my" arm or "your" leg. In other words, they do not normally use the possessive adjective, opting instead for the definite article. For example, when asking "Did you break **your** arm?" you would say *Você quebrou **o** braço?* or "Did you break **the** arm?" because it's understood that it is yours, not anyone else's.

Parts of the Body

If you do find yourself in a situation where you need to talk to a doctor, these words in Portuguese are essential. Let's say you are in a situation where you need to explain in detail a particular pain you are experiencing. Knowledge of the anatomy of the human body will prove helpful.

ankle	*o tornozelo*
	oo tohr-noh-ZEH-loo
arm	*o braço*
	oo BRAH-soo
armpit	*a axila*
	ah ahk-SEE-lah
artery	*a artéria*
	ah ahr-TEH-ree-ah
body	*o corpo*
	oo KOHR-poo
bone	*o osso*
	oo OH-soo
brain	*o cérebro*
	oo SEH-reh-broo
calf	*a batata da perna*
	ah bah-TAH-tah dah PEHR-nah
chest	*o tórax*
	oo TOH-rah-ks
collarbone	*a clavícula*
	ah klah-VEE-koo-lah
elbow	*o cotovelo*
	oo koh-toh-VEH-loo

finger	*o dedo*	
	oo DEH-doo	
foot	*o pé*	
	oo PEH	
hand	*a mão*	
	ah MAHN-oo	
heart	*o coração*	
	oo koh-rah-SAHN-oo	
heel	*o calcanhar*	
	oo kahl-kahn-NYAH	
hip	*o quadril*	
	oo kwa-DREE-oo	
index finger	*o indicador*	
	oo een-dee-kah-DOH	
knee	*o joelho*	
	oo joo-EH-lyoo	
larynx	*a laringe*	
	ah lah-REEN-zhee	
leg	*a perna*	
	ah PEHR-nah	
middle finger	*o dedo médio*	
	oo DEH-doo MEH-dee-oo	
muscle	*o músculo*	
	oo MOOS-koo-loo	
nail	*a unha*	
	ah UNH-nyah	
nerve	*o nervo*	
	oo NEHR-voo	
pinkie	*o dedo mindinho*	
	oo DEH-doo meen-DEEN-nyoo	

rib	*a costela*
	ah koohs-TEH-lah
ring finger	*o dedo anular*
	oo DEH-doo ah-noo-LAH
shoulder	*o ombro*
	oo ONH-broo
skin	*a pele*
	ah PEH-lee
spine	*a coluna; a espinha*
	ah koh-LOO-nah; ah ehs-PEEN-nyah
stomach	*o estômago*
	oo ehs-TOH-mah-goo
thumb	*o polegar; o dedão*
	oo poh-leh-GAH; oo deh-DAHN-oo
vein	*a veia*
	ah VEH-ee-ya
wrist	*o pulso*
	oo POOL-soo

Going to the Doctor

The following vocabulary, in conjunction with the common ailments section, can help you describe your symptoms to a doctor so they can diagnose you properly.

to be cold	*estar resfriado/a*
	ehs-TAH hehs-free-AH-doo/-ah
to be hot;	*ter febre*
have a fever	teh FEH-bree

to be pregnant	*estar grávida*
	ehs-TAH GRAH-vee-dah
to be sick	*estar doente*
	ehs-TAH doo-EHN-tee, tchee (variable pronunciation)
to be tired	*estar cansado/a*
	ehs-TAH kahn-SAH-doo/-dah
to have diarrhea	*ter diarréia*; *ter desinteria*
	teh dee-ah-HEH-ye-ah; teh deh-sihn-teh-REE-ah

One of the most common questions in a doctor's office is whether you have any allergies. If you suffer from an allergy, use the following expressions to relay this information to your doctor before he prescribes any medication or suggests a treatment:

I am allergic to …

Sou alérgico a … / Sou alérgica a … (male speaker, female speaker)
soh ah-LEHR-zhee-koo ah … / soh ah-LEHR-zhee-kah ah …

Tenho alergia a …
TEHN-nyoo ah-lehr-GEE-ah ah …

aspirin	*aspirina*
	ahs-pee-REE-nah
penicillin	*penicilina*
	pehn-nee-see-LEEN-nah
antibiotics	*antibióticos*
	ahn-tee-bee-OH-tee-koos

SYMPTOMATIC VERBS

to bleed	*sangrar*
	sahn-GRAH
to cough	*tossir*
	too-SEEH
to faint	*desmaiar*
	deehs-mah-yee-AH
to fall	*cair*
	kah-EEH
to sneeze	*espirrar*
	ehs-pee-HAH
to vomit	*vomitar*
	voh-mee-TAH

Going to the Hospital

If everything goes well on your trip, you won't need to go to a hospital. Accidents can happen at any time, though, even on vacation! If you do end up visiting a hospital during your travels, the following are the words and expressions you might need.

anesthetic	*o anestésico*
	oo ah-nehs-TEH-zee-koo
blood test	*o exame de sangue*
	oo eh-zahn-mee dee SAHN-ghee
blood type	*o tipo sanguíneo*
	oo TEE-poh sahn-GHEE-neh-oo
blood transfusion	*a transfusão*
	ah trahns-foo-ZAHN-oo
diagnosis	*o diagnóstico*
	oo dee-ahg-NOHS-tee-koo
(to) be discharged	*(ter) alta do hospital*
	(teh) AHL-tah doo oohs-pee-TAH-oo
doctor	*o medico/a médica*
	oo MEH-dee-koo/ah MEH-dee-kah
examination (physical)	*o exame físico*
	oo eh-ZAHN-mee FEE-zee-koo
to examine	*examinar*
	eh-zah-mee-NAH
hospital	*o hospital*
	oo OHS-pee-TAH-oo
infusion	*a infusão venosa*
	ah een-foo-SAHN-oo veh-NOH-sah
injection	*a injeção*
	ah een-geh-SAHN-oo
intensive care unit	*a UTI (unidade de terapia intensiva)*
	ah oo-teh-ee (oo-nee-DAH-dee dee teh-rah-PEE-ah een-tehn-SEE-vah)
medical director	*o director clínico*
	oo dee-reh-TOH KLEE-nee-koo

night nurse	*a enfermeira do turno da noite*
	ah een-fehr-MAY-rah doo TOOH-noo dah NOY-tee
nurse	*a enfermeira*
	ah een-fehr-MAY-rah
to operate	*operar*
	oo-peh-RAH
operation	*a operação*
	ah oh-peh-rah-SAHN-oo
patient	*o/a paciente*
	oo/ah pah-see-EHN-tee
surgeon	*o cirurgião/a cirurgiã*
	oo see-ROOH-gee-AHN-oo/ah see-ROOH-gee-AHN
temperature chart	*a curva de temperatura*
	ah KOOH-vah dah tehn-peh-rah-TOO-rah
visiting hours	*o horário de visita*
	oo oh-RAH-ree-oo dee vee-ZEE-tah
to x-ray	*tirar um raio-x*
	tee-RAH oohn HA-ye-oo sheesh

Going to the Dentist

It might be good to also familiarize yourself with the following vocabulary about teeth and dentistry—just in case you have to stop your vacation because of a toothache. It might happen, so make sure you are ready to explain it to the dentist. You will notice that Brazilian dentists function very much the same way that U.S. dentists do, with very little change in dental care. In fact, you might experience an even better service for relatively less costly procedures.

at the dentist's office	*no dentista*
	noo dehn-TEES-tah
tooth	*o dente*
	oo DEHN-tee
abscess	*o abcesso*
	oo ahb-SEH-soo
local anesthesia	*a anestesia local*
	ah ah-nehs-teh-ZEE-ah loh-KAHL
molar	*o molar*
	oo moh-LAH
braces	*o aparelho ortodôntico*
	oo ah-pah-REH-lyoo ohr-toh-DOHN-tee-koo
bridge	*a ponte*
	ah POHN-tee
cavity	*a cárie*
	ah KAH-ree-yeh
crown	*a coroa*
	ah koh-ROH-ah
cuspid	*o canino*
	oo kah-NEE-noo
dental clinic	*a clínica dentária*
	ah KLEE-nee-kah dehn-TAH-ree-ah
denture	*a dentadura*
	ah dehn-tah-DOO-rah
to extract	*estrair*
	ehs-TRAH-eer
false tooth	*a prótese*
	ah PROH-teh-zee
fill	*obturar*
	ohb-too-RAH

filling	*a obturação*
	ah ohb-too-rah-SAHN-oo
gums	*a gengiva*
	ah jehn-JEE-vah
incisor	*o incisivo*
	oo een-see-ZEE-voh
injection	*a injeção*
	ah een-jeh-SAHN-oo
jaw	*a mandíbula*
	ah mahn-DEE-boo-lah
nerve	*o nervo*
	oo NEHR-voh
oral surgeon	*o cirurgião oral*
	oo see-rooh-jee-AHN-oo oh-RAH-oo
orthodontist	*o ortodontista*
	oo ohr-toh-dohn-TEES-tah
plaster cast	*o modelo de gesso*
	oo moh-DEH-loo dee GEH-soo
root	*a raiz*
	ah HA-ees
root canal work	*o tratamento de canal*
	oo trah-tah-MEHN-too dee kah-NAH-oo
tartar	*o tártaro*
	oo TAHR-tah-roo
temporary filling	*a obturação provisória*
	ah ohb-too-rah-SAHN-oo proh-vee-SOH-ree-ah
toothache	*a dor de dente*
	ah DOHR dee DEHN-tee
wisdom tooth	*o dente de siso*
	oo DEHN-tee dee SEE-zoo

A FEW DENTAL VERBS

to bleed	*sangrar*
	sahn-GRAH
to brush one's teeth	*escovar os dentes*
	ehs-koh-VAH oos DEHN-tees
to lose a tooth	*perder um dente*
	pehr-DEH oohn DEHN-tee
to pull out; remove	*estrair*
	ehs-trah-EEH
to rinse	*fazer um bochecho*
	fah-ZEH oohn boh-SHEH-shoo

Going to the Pharmacy

Perhaps the doctor you visit will prescribe some medication for your ailment or recommend an over-the-counter remedy. In Brazil, pharmacies are numerous, and they carry many cosmetic items, such as local stores in the United States. You might be able to get your remedies, as well as shampoo and skin care products. The following words will help you get what you need in a pharmacy.

pharmacy	*a farmácia*
	ah fahr-MAH-see-yah
pharmacist	*o farmacêutico/a farmacêutica*
	oo fahr-mah-SEH-oo-tee-koo/
	ah fahr-mah-SEH-oo-tee-kah

ace bandage	*a faixa; a atadura*
	ah FAH-yee-shah; ah ah-tah-DOO-rah
adhesive bandage	*o curativo; o band-aid*
	oo koo-rah-TEE-voo; oo bahn-DEY-dee
aspirin	*a aspirina*
	ah ahs-pee-REE-nah
cough syrup	*o xarope*
	oo shah-ROH-pee
digestive tonic	*o tônico digestivo*
	oo TOHN-nee-koo dee-gehs-TEE-voo
disinfectant	*o desinfetante*
	oo deh-zeen-feh-TAHN-tee
drops	*as gotas*
	ahs GO-tahs
gauze bandage	*a faixa de gaze*
	ah FAH-yee-shah dee GAH-zee
insect repellant	*o repelente*
	ooh heh-peh-LEHN-tee
laxative	*o laxante*
	oo lah-SHAHN-tee
medicine	*o remédio; o medicamento*
	oo heh-MEH-dee-oo; oo meh-dee-kah-MEHN-too
pill	*o comprimido*
	oo kohn-pree-MEE-doo
(birth control) pill	*a pílula (anticoncepcional)*
	ah PEE-loo-lah (ahn-tee-kohn-sep-see-oh-NAHL)
prescription	*a receita (médica); a prescrição*
	ah heh-SEY-tah (MEH-dee-kah);
	ah prehs-kree-SAHN-oo

prophylactics	*o preservativo; a camisinha* (colloquial)
	oo preh-zeh-vah-TEE-voo; ah kahn-mee-ZEEN-ah
remedy	*o remédio*
	ooh heh-MEH-dee-oo
thermometer	*o termômetro*
	oo tehr-MOHN-meh-troo
tranquilizer	*o tranquilizante*
	oo trahn-kwee-lee-ZAHN-tee
vaseline	*a vaselina*
	ah vah-zee-LEE-nah

 Alert

Most Brazilians will simply use the word *a pílula* to refer to the birth control pill. Others will simply use the word *anticoncepcional*. Either way, a woman would need a prescription to purchase it. The common word for condom is *camisinha* "little shirt" as described above.

Emergencies and Disasters

It's more than likely you will never need to know any vocabulary relating to emergencies or disasters, but here are a few key words and phrases you can use on the off chance that you run into unforeseen trouble.

Help!	*Socorro!*
	soo-KO-hoo
Police!	*Polícia!*
	poh-LEE-see-yah

Thief!	*Ladrão!*
	lah-DRAHN-oo
Watch out!	*Cuidado!*
	koo-yee-DAH-doo
accident	*um acidente*
	oohn ah-see-DEHN-tee
attack	*um ataque*
	oohn ah-TAH-kee
burglary	*um furto*
	oohn FOOH-too
fire	*um incêndio*
	oohn een-SEHN-dee-yo
flood	*uma enchente*
	oohn-ah ehn-SHEN-tee
gunshot	*um tiro*
	oohn TEE-roo
rape	*o estupro*
	oo ehs-TOO-proh
ambulance	*a ambulância*
	ah ahn-boo-LAHN-see-yah

CHAPTER 11

In Your Community

Let's say that instead of just a few days, you decided to stay in Brazil for a longer period of time. You will need to take care of the unavoidable day-to-day errands and chores. The following will give you the common terms and expressions for your everyday interactions with store owners, local businesses, and people in the community. Don't forget, Brazilians are very receptive to outsiders who make an effort to speak their language!

At the Market

Food shopping in Brazilian cities can be a fun and interesting experience. You will find supermarkets (very similar to their American counterparts) pretty much everywhere. Many Brazilians, however, get essentials at bakeries or perhaps at the local market.

bakery	*a padaria*
	ah pah-dah-REE-ah
book shop	*a livraria*
	ah lee-vrah-REE-ah
butcher shop	*o açougue*
	oo ah-SO-ghee
market	*o mercado*
	oo mehr-KAH-doo
department store	*a loja de departamento*
	ah LOH-jah dee deh-pahr-tah-MEHN-too
fishmonger	*a peixaria*
	ah pay-shah-REE-ah
florist	*o florista*
	oo floh-REES-tah
grocery store	*o supermercado*
	oo soo-pehr-mehr-KAH-doo
hardware store	*a loja de ferragens*
	ah LOH-jah dee feh-HAH-gehns
jewelry store	*a joalheria*
	ah joh-ahl-yeh-REE-ah
newsstand	*a banca de revista*
	ah BAHN-kah dee heh-VEES-tah

paper store	*a papelaria*
	ah pah-peh-lah-REE-ah
pastry shop	*a pastelaria*
	ah pahs-teh-lah-REE-ah
perfume store	*a perfumaria*
	ah pehr-foo-mah-REE-ah
pharmacy	*a farmácia*; *a drogaria*
	ah fahr-MAH-see-ya; ah droh-gah-REE-a
supermarket	*o supermercado*
	oo soo-pehr-mehr-KAH-doo
toy store	*a loja de brinquedos*
	ah LOH-jah dee breen-KEH-doos

 Fact

An older word for market is *mercearia* (mehr-sheh-ah-REE-ah), which is only used in rural areas and by older folks. The most common word for a grocery store is *supermercado* (soo-pehr-mehr-KAH-doo). This is a much larger grocery store that is common in big cities.

IN THE SHOP

cash register	*o caixa*
	oo KAH-ye-shah
closed	*fechado*
	feh-SHAH-doo
entrance	*entrada*
	ehn-TRAH-dah

exit	*saída*
	sah-EE-dah
sale	*o saldo*; *a liquidação*
	oo SAHL-doo; ah lee-kee-dah-SAHN-oo
special offer	*a oferta*
	ah oh-FEHR-tah
open	*aberto*
	ah-BEHR-too
opening hours	*horário de atendimento*
	oh-RAH-ree-oo dee ah-tehn-dee-MEHN-too

Quantities, Weights, and Measures

Knowing the correct terms for quantities, weights, and measures can be very helpful when you are out shopping for food. Street markets in Brazil are normally crowded, so it is important to be aware of your surroundings. Here are some words that you might need to know while shopping there.

How much does it weigh? It weighs … kilograms.
Quanto pesa? Pesa . . . quilos.
KAHWN-too PEH-zah? PEH-zah …KEE-loos

bit; piece	*um pouco*; *um pedaço*
	oohn POH-koo; oohn peh-DAH-soo
bottle	*uma garrafa*
	oohn-ah gah-HAH-fah

box	*uma caixa*
	oohn-ah KAH-ye-shah
can	*uma lata*
	oohn-ah LAH-tah
jar	*um pote*
	oohn POH-tee
gram	*um grama*
	oohn GRAHN-mah
kilogram	*um quilo*
	oohn KEE-loo
liter	*um litro*
	oohn LEE-troh

 Alert

When ordering food items by weight, you are more likely to express that weight using kilograms (*quilos*). For example, *um quilo de carne* would be exactly 2.2 pounds of beef. Usually Brazilians order half a kilo or one kilo. If your order is less than a quarter of a kilo, then say 250 grams (*duzentos e cinquenta gramas*, doo-ZEHN-toos ee seen-KWEN-tah GRAHN-mahs), and so forth.

enough	*é suficiente*; *tá bom* (colloquial)
	eh soo-fee-see-EHN-tee; TAH bohn
more	*mais*
	MAH-yees
less; fewer	*menos*
	MEHN-noos

a little	*um pouco de . . .*
	oohn POH-koo dee . . .
too much; too many	*muito*; *demais*
	MOOHN-yeen-too; dee-MAH-yees

 Alert

Visiting the street markets or *feiras* (FEY-rahs) are a great way to experience Brazil. You will find arts and crafts, fruits and vegetables, among many other local items at those places. Carry only enough money with you to make your purchases, have a copy of your passport (not the original), and make sure to carry your purse or backpack in front of you (this makes it more difficult for pickpockets to take items from it).

At the Bakery or Coffee Shop

In Brazil you will find that people do a daily run to the bakery to get bread, especially if they live in smaller cities. There are bakeries on almost every street corner, and coffee shops or snack bars are usually connected to the bakery shops in the same building. This way, you can easily have a *cafezinho* (espresso, strong coffee) and eat a pastry while reading the paper, then buy bread for the evening meal.

(small) coffee	*um cafezinho*
	oohn kah-feh-ZEEN-nyoo
a glass of orange juice	*um suco de laranja*
	oohn SOO-koo dee lah-RAHN-jah
a piece of cake	*um pedaço de bolo*
	oohn peh-DAH-soo dee BOH-loo
cake	*bolo*
	BOH-loo
chocolate	*chocolate*
	shoh-koh-LAH-tee
coffee	*café*
	kah-FEH
cookie	*biscoito*
	bees-KOY-too
fruit pie	*torta de fruta*
	TOHR-tah dee FROO-tah
ice cream	*sorvete*
	sorh-VEH-tee
chocolate ice cream	*sorvete de chocolate*
	sorh-VEH-tee dee shoh-koh-LAH-tee
strawberry ice cream	*sorvete de morango*
	sorh-VEH-tee dee moh-RAHN-goo
vanilla ice cream	*sorvete de baunilha*
	sorh-VEH-tee dee bah-oo-NEE-lyah
sugar	*o açúcar*
	oo ah-SOO-kah
sweets	*os doces*
	oohs-DOH-sees
whipped cream	*o crème chantilly*
	oo KREH-mee shan-tee-LEE

Fact

There are many tropical fruit flavors of ice cream that you can try in Brazil, so don't just stick with the traditional flavors such as chocolate, strawberry, and vanilla. Try coconut, avocado, pineapple, mango, etc. There are also fruits you might have never even heard of, such as *pinha* and *graviola*. *Pinha* looks like a pine cone; it's green on the outside and has a white, meaty center, with plenty of little tiny black stones. You can eat it just as is. *Graviola* is also found in Mexico and it is about the size of a winter squash, except it is green and prickly on the outside. Inside you have the edible white part that is too tart to eat without sugar.

At the Post Office

Os Correios in Brazil is a federally funded company that provides mailing services for letters, packages, telegrams, and other support, including bill payment and registering as a taxpayer. If there is a sign that says *banco postal*, you can be sure that certain bank services are available at that post office. The decision to include bank services at post offices came from a government that supported initiatives to be more socially inclusive. The post office is generally open Monday to Friday from 9:00 A.M. to 5:00 P.M. and on Saturdays from 9:00 A.M. to 1:00 P.M.

address	*o endereço*
	oo ehn-deh-REH-soo
addressee	*o destinatário*
	oo dehs-tee-nah-TAH-ree-oo
air mail	*correio aéreo*
	koh-HEH-yoo ah-EH-reh-oo
counter	*o caixa de atendimento*
	oo KAH-yee-shah dee ah-tehn-dee-MEHN-too
customs declaration	*a declaração aduaneira*
	ah deh-klah-rah-SAHN-oo ah-doo-ah-NEY-rah
destination	*o destino*
	oo dehs-TEE-noo
document tracking	*rastreamento de documentos*
	hahs-treh-ah-MEHN-too dee doh-koo-MEHN-toos
information	*a informação*
	ah een-fohr-MAH-sahn-oo
letter	*a carta*
	ah KAHR-tah
lost and found	*achados e perdidos*
	ah-SHAH-doos ee pehr-DEE-doos
mailbox	*a caixa de correio*
	ah KAH-ye-shah dee koh-HEY-yoo
package	*uma encomenda; um pacote*
	oohn-ah ehn-koh-MEHN-dah; oohn pah-KOH-tee
postage	*a franquia*
	ah frahn-KEE-ah
postal clerk	*o funcionário dos correios*
	oo foohn-see-oh-NAH-ree-oo doohs koh-HEY-yoos
postcard	*o cartão postal*
	oo kahr-TAHN-oo pohs-TAH-oo

post office box	*a caixa postal*
	ah KAH-ye-shah pohs-TAH-oo
postman	*o carteiro* (usually a male profession)
	oo kahr-TEH-ye-roo
printed matter	*o impresso*
	oo een-PREH-soo
receipt	*o recibo*
	ooh heh-SEE-boo
to register	*fazer uma matrícula*
	fah-ZEH oohn-ah mah-TREE-koo-lah
registered letter	*uma carta registrada*
	oohn-ah KAHR-tah heh-jees-TRAH-dah
sender	*o remetente*
	oh heh-meh-TEHN-tee
special delivery	*encomenda especial*
	ehn-koh-MEHN-dah ehs-peh-SEE-al
stamp (noun)	*o selo*
	oo SEH-loo
to stamp	*selar*
	seh-LAH
stamp machine	*a máquina de franquear*
	ah MAH-kee-nah dee frahn-kee-AH
telegram	*o telegrama*
	oo teh-leh-GRAH-mah
unstamped	*sem selo*
	sehn SEH-loo
value declaration	*a declaração do valor*
	ah deh-klah-rah-SAHN-oo doo vah-LOH

 **Essential**

Depending on the region of the country, some post office stores open at 8 A.M. You have to make sure to check the hours before you go. It is also true that they are open on Saturday afternoons, but only until 1 P.M. They are closed on Sundays.

Weather Words and Expressions

Brazil is a tropical country, even if some parts of it can be more temperate. Depending on where and when you visit Brazil, you will need to know a number of weather expressions. If you're out and about and the weather starts to change, this section will help you come up with the correct words and terms.

How's the weather?
Como está o tempo?
KOH-moo ehs-TAH oo TEHN-poo

WEATHER EXPRESSIONS	
It's sunny.	*Faz sol.*
	fah-yees SOHL
It's nice.	*O tempo está bom.*
	oo TEHN-poo ehs-TAH bohn
It's cold.	*Faz frio.*
	fah-yees FREE-oo

WEATHER EXPRESSIONS (*CONTINUED*)

It's hot.	*Faz calor, Está quente.*
	fah-yees kah-LOH; ehs-TAH KEHN-tee
It's snowing.	*Está nevando.*
	ehs-TAH neh-VAHN-doo
It's raining.	*Está chovendo.*
	ehs-TAH shoo-VEHN-doo
It's windy.	*Está ventando.*
	ehs-TAH vehn-TAHN-doo
It's foggy.	*É nebuloso.*
	eh neh-boo-LOH-zoo
storm	*a tempestade*
	ah tehn-pehs-TAH-dee
lightning	*o relâmpago*
	oo heh-LAHN-pah-goo
changeable	*variável*
	vah-ree-AH-veh-oo
rain	*a chuva*
	ah SHOO-vah
barometer	*o barômetro*
	oo bah-ROH-meh-troo
to rain	*chover*
	shoh-VEH
blizzard	*a tormenta*
	ah tohr-MEHN-tah
snow	*a neve*
	ah NEH-vee
climate	*o clima*
	oo KLEE-mah

Alert

Brazil has many climate areas, from tropical to sub-tropical. The weather tends to be colder in the southern states of Paraná and Santa Catarina and hotter and more humid in the northern parts of the country, such as Bahia and Ceará. Because the country is south of the Equator, seasons are the exact opposite as in the United States. Thus, it is probably better to plan a visit during the cooler, Brazilian winter months of June, July, and August. The weather is normally milder and there are fewer tourists during those months.

WEATHER EXPRESSIONS (*CONTINUED*)

cloud	*a nuvem*
	ah NOO-vehn
sun	*o sol*
	oo SOHL
rainstorm	*o temporal*
	oo tehn-poh-RAH-oo
cloudy	*nublado*
	noo-BLAH-doo
dusk	*o crepúsculo*
	oo kreh-POOS-koo-loh
fog	*a neblina*
	ah neh-BLEEN-nah
frost	*a geada*
	ah zheh-AH-dah

WEATHER EXPRESSIONS (*CONTINUED*)

hail	*o granizo*
	oo grah-NEE-zoo
ice	*o gelo*
	oo JEH-loo
mist	*a névoa*
	ah NEH-voh-ah
weather report	*o boletim metereológico*
	oo boh-leh-TEEN meh-teh-reh-oh-LOH-jee-koo

CHAPTER 12

Brazilian Portuguese in the Digital World

If you love to use social media sites to share your vacation photos or update your friends on your location, the following sections will help you learn the most common words that deal with the Internet and computers in Portuguese. Although some of these words are of English origin, some are not. You will also get a summary of common Brazilian idiomatic expressions that will be very useful to you as a foreign visitor, as well as words that will be helpful when using social media sites such as Facebook. Finally, you will learn what you always wanted to say in Portuguese, but your teacher never taught you!

Computers and the Internet

The Internet has changed our lives profoundly. It is now part of how people advertise, conduct business, interact, and meet others. Thanks to sites like Facebook, Twitter, and Tumblr, social media has become an essential tool for travelers. If you plan on using a computer during your vacation, knowledge of terms associated with computing and the Internet will most certainly be important on your trip.

 Fact

You will find that many English words have found their way into the Portuguese language. This is especially true with words related to computer technology. However, it must be stated that although these words are spelled exactly the same as in English, Brazilians pronounce them following a Portuguese sound pattern. Make sure to check the pronunciation guides in this chapter.

(e-mail) address	*o endereço (eletrônico)*
	oo ehn-deh-REH-soo eh-leh-TROH-nee-koo
browser	*o navegador*
	oo nah-veh-gah-DOH
to click	*clicar*
	klee-KAH
computer	*o computador*
	oo kohn-poo-tah-DOH
control panel	*o painel de controle*
	oo pah-ee-NEHL dee kohn-TROH-lee

dialogue box	*a janela de diálogo*
	ah jah-NEH-la dee dee-AH-loh-goo
to download	*baixar*
	bah-ee-SHAH
folder	*o arquivo*
	oo ahr-KEE-voo
hyperlink	*o linque (or o link)*
	oo LEEN-kee
icon	*o ícone*
	oo EE-koh-nee
folder	*a pasta de trabalho*
	ah PAHS-tah dee trah-BAH-lyoo
Internet	*o internete; a rede*
	oo een-tehr-NEH-tee; ah REH-dee
keyboard	*o teclado*
	oo teh-KLAH-doo
keywords	*as palavras-chave*
	ahs pah-LAH-vrahs SHAH-vees
to be online	*estar online*
	ehs-TAH ohn-LAH-ee-nee
operating system	*o sistema de operação*
	oo sees-TEH-mah dee oh-peh-rah-SAHN-oo
page	*a página*
	ah PAH-jee-nah
password	*a senha*
	ah SEHN-nyah
printer	*a impressora*
	ah een-preh-SOH-rah
to reboot	*fazer o reboot*
	fah-ZEH oo hee-BOO-tee

to restart	*ligar e desligar*
	leeh-GAH ee dehs-lee-GAH
search engine	*o motor de busca*
	oo moh-TOH dee BOOS-kah
site	*o site*
	oo SAH-ee-teh
system folder	*a pasta do sistema*
	ah PAHS-tah do sees-TEH-mah

Social Media Language

The world has changed significantly in the last few years since the advent of Facebook, Twitter, and other social media sites. In this section, you will learn common words that have more recently entered Brazilian society and the Portuguese language.

FACEBOOK/TWITTER LANGUAGE	
ENGLISH	**PORTUGUESE**
Facebook	o "Face"/ o "Facebook"
	oo FEY-see/ oo FEY-see-BOO-kee
Twitter	o "Twitter" / o "Tuiter"
	oo too-EE-tehr
to tag	*fazer o "tag"*
	fah-ZEH oo TEH-ghee
to "like"	*curtir*
	koohr-TEEH
to post	*postar*
	pohs-TAH

FACEBOOK/TWITTER LANGUAGE (CONTINUED)

ENGLISH	PORTUGUESE
to comment	*comentar*
	kohn-mehn-TAH
to message	*mandar mensagem*
	manh-DAH mehn-SAH-jehn
to add (a friend)	*adicionar*
	ah-dee-see-oh-NAH
change your "status"	*mudar o teu "status"*
	moo-DAH oo teh-oo ehs-TAH-toos
to upload	*fazer o "upload"*
	fah-ZEH oo ah-pee-LO-dee
to download	*baixar*
	bah-ee-SHAH
followers	*seguidores*
	seh-ghee-DOH-rees

Here are some examples of expressions you might read on Facebook or Twitter in Brazilian Portuguese:

Are you going to friend me on Facebook?
Você vai me adicionar no Feice?
voh-SAY VAH-ee mee ah-dee-see-oh-NAH noo FEY-see

Who is going to post first?
Quem vai postar primeiro?
KEHN-ee VAH-ee pohs-TAH pree-MEY-roo

Did you "like" my comment?

Você curtiu meu comentário?

voh-SAY koohr-TEE-oo meh-oo kohn-mehn-TAH-ree-oo

Are you going to send that Twitter message?/Are you going to tweet that?

Você vai mandar aquele tuiter?/ Vai tuitar aquilo?

voh-SAY vah-ee mahn-DAH ah-KEH-lee too-EE-tehr/
VAH-ee too-ee-TAH ah-KEE-loo

How many followers do you have?

Quantos seguidores você tem?

kwan-toos seh-ghee-DOH-rees voh-SAY tehn-ee

 **Essential**

Brazilians do not say the entire word "Facebook"; they shorten it to "Face" (pronounced FEY-see) and it is often written as *Feice*. That is how Brazilians would write the word, following a Portuguese sound system. Since this is all very new, you might see variable spelling, such as "to twitter" being *tuitar* (too-ee-TAH).

These days many Brazilians have smart phones, on which you can check your email messages, check social media sites, and post comments. Sending text messages is also very common. These are called *torpedos* (tohr-PEH-doos).

She sent me about forty text messages yesterday.
Ela me mandou uns quarenta torpedos ontem.
EH-lah mee mahn-DOH uhns kwah-REHN-tah tohr-PEH-doos OHN-tenh-ee

Common Idiomatic Expressions

The following expressions apply to a great variety of situations and are commonly used and understood throughout Brazil. Most can be used in both formal and informal situations.

Não me diga!	You don't say!
NAHN-oo mee DEE-gah	
a todo custo	at any cost; no matter what
ah TOH-doo KOOS-too	
Tá combinado.	It's a deal.
tah kohn-bee-NAH-doo	
Já era hora!	It's about time!
JAH EH-rah OH-rah	
Podes crer!	Of course; You can bet your life!
POH-dees kreh	
Que sorte!	How lucky (for you)!
kee SOHR-tee	
Que saco!	How boring!
kee SAH-koo	
Que confusão!	What a mess!
kee kohn-foo-SAHN-oo	

Que chato!	How boring!
kee SHAH-too	
Não acredito!	I can't believe it!
NAHN-oo ah-kreh-DEE-too	
Que nojo!	How disgusting!
kee NOH-joo	
Deus o livre!	God forbid!
DEH-oos oo LEE-vree	
por outro lado . . .	on the other hand . . .
pohr ROW-troo LAH-doo	
Demais da conta!	A lot!
dee-MAH-ees dah KOHN-tah	
É mesmo?	Really?
EH MEHS-moo	
entenda que . . .	bear in mind . . .
ehn-TEHN-dah keh...	
entre outras . . .	among other things . . .
EHN-tree OH-trahs pah-LAH-vrahs	
de qualquer modo	anyway; at any cost
dee kwal-KHER MOH-doo	
em poucas palavras	in a few words
ehn POH-kahs pah-LAH-vrahs	
Esquece! Deixa pra lá!	Forget it!
ehs-KEH-see! DEY-shah prah LAH	
Me esquece!	Leave me alone!
mee ehs-KEH-see	
Nem sonhando!	Not even in your dreams!
nehn sohn-NYAHN-doo	

Melhor assim.	It's better this way.
meh-lee-OH ah-SEEN	
Melhor que nada.	Better than nothing at all.
meh-lee-OH kee NAH-dah	
Ainda bem!	Luckily!
ah-EEN-dah BEHN-ee	
Não aguento mais.	I can't take it anymore.
NAHN-oo ah-GWEHN-too MAH-ees	
hoje em dia	nowadays
OH-jee ehn DEE-ah	
Ave Maria!	Mother of God!
AH-veh mah-REE-ah	
em suma	to cut it short
ehn SOO-mah	
Putz!	Damn it!
POO-tees	
Que loucura!	That's crazy!
kee loh-KOO-rah	
Tem certeza?	Are you sure?
tehn-ee sehr-TEH-zah	
Com certeza!	For sure!
kohn sehr-TEH-zah	
É sério?	Really?
eh SEH-ree-oo	
bem melhor	so much the better
behn-ee meh-lee-OH	
bem pior	so much the worse
behn-ee pee-OH	

esteja ciente . . .	keep in mind . . .
ehs-TEH-jah see-EHN-tee	
pelo contrário	on the contrary
PEH-loo kohn-TRAH-ree-oo	
Valhe a pena.	It's worth it.
VAH-lee-ye ah PEHN-nah	

 Essential

It's not as hard to learn idiomatic expressions or phrases as you might think. Certainly the locals use them often enough. The trick is to know what is said before and after those idiomatic expressions. That takes a lot more sophisticated understanding of the language as a whole. Keep practicing your Portuguese, rent Brazilian movies, listen to Brazilian music, and ask as many questions as you can (to those who are bilingual).

What Your Portuguese Teacher Never Taught You

The following list is by no means complete, nor is it rife with vulgarities. It does contain some fun and colorful expressions to be used in a variety of situations.

amor a primeira vista	love at first sight
ah-MOHR ah pree-MEY-rah VEES-tah	
encher o saco	to annoy someone
ehn-SHEH oo SAH-koo	

estar de saco cheio	to be fed up
ehs-TAH dee SAH-koo SHEY-oo	
Ai, que saco!	How annoying!
AH-ee kee SAH-koo	
ficar com tesão	to become sexually excited
fee-KAH kohn teh-SAHN-oo	
encher a cara	to get drunk
ehn-SHEH ah KAH-rah	
tomar um porre	to get really drunk
toh-MAH oohn POH-hee	
estar de ressaca	to be hungover
ehs-TAH dee heh-SAH-kah	
Tá ligado?	You get me? You know what I'm saying?
tah lee-GAH-doo	
Ficou louco?	You crazy?
fee-KO LOH-koo	
Não entra nessa!	Don't be fooled!
nahn-oo EHN-trah NEH-sah	
Se cuida!	Take care of yourself!
see KOO-ye-dah	
Me poupe!	Give me a break!
mee PO-pee	
Ela é gostosa.	She's sexually attactive.
eh-lah EH gohs-TOH-zah	
Ele é um gato!	He's gorgeous! (literally: he's a cat)
eh-lee EH oohn GAH-too	
Ele é um tesão!	He is sexually attractive!
eh-lee EH oohn teh-SAHN-oo	
Cale a boca!	Shut up!
KAH-lee ah BOH-kah	

puxa-saco POO-shah SAH-koo	brownnoser
morrer de tédio moo-HEH dee TEH-dee-oo	to die of boredom
palavrão pah-lah-VRANH-oo	bad/dirty word
Que loucura! kee lo-KOO-rah	How crazy!
Que nojo! kee NO-joo	How gross!

 **Essential**

If you hear an expression you don't understand, make sure you ask for clarification, or write it down so you can look it up later. Brazilian Portuguese can be a very colorful language, so make sure you get all the inside jokes!

CHAPTER 13

Overview of Brazilian Culture

Brazilians love to celebrate. If you are lucky enough to travel to Brazil during one of its popular events, such as *Carnaval*, you will experience the excitement of Brazilian culture firsthand. This chapter covers the Brazilian feast of *Carnaval* and the love for food, music, and soccer shared by many Brazilians. You will learn about the origins of unique musical expressions, an incredible feast for the senses, and which are the best spots to visit in Brazil!

Brazilian *Carnaval*

This "feast" of music and dance traditionally lasts several days in mid-February. The name comes from the Latin words *carne* meaning "meat" or "flesh," and *vale*, meaning "ball" or "feast." This was the time when Catholics would enjoy eating and drinking excessively just before the Lent period. *Carnaval* continues to be a "feast of excesses," but its original religious nature has been lost to many Brazilians and Latin Americans.

 Fact

The tradition of *Carnaval* celebration started with the seventeenth century Portuguese folkloric practice called *entrudo* when, during the weeks before Lent, people would throw eggs, water, or flour at passersby in the streets. The custom was based in mischief and fun, much like many other European traditions where tomatoes or oranges are thrown at people at the end of the harvest.

As a colonial country, Brazil was very much affected and influenced by other traditions originating in France and Italy, where *Carnaval* signified urban parades, with typical characters such as the *Pierrot*, the *Colombine*, and the *Rei Momo*, the King of *Carnaval*. During the nineteenth century, the first *corsos* or decorated car parades would appear. Groups of people would decorate their cars and parade in the streets singing and dancing. These became more popular in the beginning of the twentieth century, and in Brazil the *escolas de samba* or "samba schools" were organized.

One of the first *escolas de samba* in Brazil was called *Deixa Falar* (literally meaning "Let Speak"), which later became known as *Estácio de Sá*, after a locality in Rio. Schools were later organized into a *Liga de Escolas de Samba* or a "League of Samba Schools," which regulated the *Carnaval* parade in Rio. People wanted to know which school had the best performance, the most animated group of people, the best musical emsemble, the best costumes, and so on. Nowadays the *Desfile de Carnaval* or "*Carnaval* parade" in Rio de Janeiro lasts two days and follows a complicated set of rules. "*Carnaval* judges" rate the schools based on several artistic and musical categories. Each year the winner has bragging rights until the next *Carnaval* season!

Along with samba schools, *cordões* and *bloco*s *carnavalescos* developed, in which groups of people would dress alike and march along singing, drinking, and dancing. These became increasingly popular with the addition of music that was being composed and played called the *marchinhas carnavalescas* or "little *Carnaval* songs."

Carnaval Beyond Rio and São Paulo

In the northeastern cities of Recife and Olinda, the *Carnaval* tradition is not based on *samba* but rather on more local musical styles, namely the *frevo*, which is a frenetic, rhythmic sound, and the *maracatu*, an African-based musical and dance tradition that includes elaborate costumes and a distinctive staccato beat.

In the city of Salvador, in the state of Bahia, the *trios elétricos* are basically large trucks that have been adapted to include a top platform with musicians that play a more electric *samba* sound, amplified by huge speakers that make up most of the sides of the truck. People dance around these trucks and sing along with famous Brazilian musical performers. The *trios elétricos* are a show in and of themselves.

 **Essential**

Salvador is known for its strong African connection, and many black musical groups, such as the *Olodum*, *Ileyaê*, and the *Afoxé Filhos de Ghandi* have put Brazil on the map as far as world music is concerned. If you want to hear a disctintive "black" sound in Brazil, check out these musical groups.

In Rio de Janeiro, the biggest parade of *samba* schools happens in the *Sambódromo*, a place especially built for people to admire the parade. During *Carnaval* this is primetime entertainment on TV, since the schools are judged on a series of factors, such as overall originality, songs, costumes, dancing, and performance quality.

The Music of Brazil

Brazil is the birthplace of *samba*, a highly rhythmic, melodious, and lively musical expression. It is also a dance, often performed during *Carnaval*. The *samba* sound has its origins or roots in the African tradition in Brazil. The slaves brought not only the instruments (*agogô*, *cuíca*) but also the syncopated rhythms and gyrating dance moves.

Instruments

The unique *samba* sound is achieved through an array of interesting instruments. Possibly the most well-known musical elements in *samba* are the *pandeiro*, a larger version of the tambourine, and the *cuíca*, a drum-like instrument that produces a squeaky sound, very typical of *samba* songs. Here is a list of some other *samba* instruments and their descriptions:

- *agogô*: two bells together, which are struck with a stick or squeezed together
- *caixa*: a smaller drum with strings in the bottom that creates a sound like a snare drum
- *cavaquinho*: a small, four-string, guitar-like instrument created in Portugal that later inspired the ukulele
- *chucalho*: a shaker instrument made by putting metal cans together and filling them with rocks, sand, or beans
- *cuíca*: a drum-like instrument with a stiff string inside, upon which the player slides his fingers up and down to produce a squeaky sound; the quality of the sound

can change depending on how fast you slide and pressure put on the skin of the drum

- *pandeiro*: larger version of the tambourine, which is played fast, and sometimes spun on one finger for show
- *repenique*: a medium-size drum, larger than a snare drum, that is played with a stick and one hand
- *surdo*: a very big drum that has a low but loud sound (*surdo* means "deaf" in Portuguese)
- *tamborim*: a very small, short drum, without bells or metal parts, that is played very fast with a stick

Types of *Samba*

Like many other musical genres, the *samba* has many subcategories. Aside from the *samba enredo*, the kind of fast, highly rhythmic *samba* performed during *Carnaval*, there are other slower versions of *samba*. One of the most famous is the *samba canção* or "samba song." These are slower *samba* pieces with romantic lyrics that are put to music and performed by traditional crooners. The *pagode*, which came into being in Rio and has been reproduced in other parts of Brazil, is the kind of *samba* sound that originated in the Brazilian backyards from people getting together and playing the various *samba* instruments for hours on end. All of these *samba* parties had the obligatory *cerveja* (beer) or *cachaça* (sugarcane rum) that came with a traditional party. There is a good amount of humor in the lyrics, which makes them extremely popular.

For more information about *samba*, check out *www.worldsamba.org*.

Bossa Nova

Brazil is not famous just for *samba*. There are several musical expressions that can trace their roots back to the country of Carmen Miranda. One of the most popular is *bossa nova*. This musical expression was started in the late fifties by upper middle class composers. It is a jazzy musical style that emphasizes the carefree living so typical of the Rio de Janeiro beach scene. For that very reason *bossa nova* was criticized, because it bore very little resemblance to the life of working class Brazilians, as many of the *samba* lyrics would have. One of the most famous *bossa nova* songs is *A Garota de Ipanema* ("The Girl from Ipanema") by Antonio Carlos Jobim. This song is nothing more than a description of a beautiful woman walking to the beach. It's about the sweet way she moves and the sentiment of the composer, who confesses that she is the most beautiful thing that he has ever seen go by. The song became known to American audiences when Frank Sinatra recorded its English version and is known all over the world as one of the most recognized Brazilian tunes.

Música Popular Brasileira or "Brazilian Popular Music"

Also called "*MPB*" for short, this type of song grew out of the Brazilian protest songs of the sixties. This musical style can be traced to a strong reaction against the carefree lyrics of *bossa nova*. After the military coup of 1964, *MPB* artists strived to put the harsh reality of Brazilian life front and center. One of the songs that clearly depicts working class Brazilians is *Pedro Pedreiro* by Chico Buarque de

Hollanda. The song is a wonderfully written narration of the monotonous life of a bricklayer. Other famous *MPB* singers and composers include Milton Nascimento, Caetano Veloso, and Gilberto Gil. Veloso and others created the psychedelic musical style of the seventies called *Tropicália*, which added to the richness of musical styles of the time. *MPB* is part of the Brazilian music scene to this day, with an incredible array of female interpreters, such as Maria Bethânia, Marisa Monte, Ana Carolina, and many others. Do not be surprised if you are invited to a party and one of the guests pulls out a guitar, starts a tune, and is joined by several other guests in singing well-known *MPB* lyrics.

Música Sertaneja: Brazil's Answer to Country Music

In contrast to *samba* and *bossa nova*, which are truly urban styles of music, *música sertaneja* has its origin in the interior or back country of Brazil. It has similarities to American country music, in that the lyrics reflect romantic themes and the plight of cowboys. It can be associated with the uneducated class, but the record sales of *sertaneja* songsters are a testament to its popularity.

Brazilian Classical Music

Perhaps people do not normally associate Brazil with classical music, but classical musicians are very familiar with the music of famous Brazilian classical composers. Two of the most famous ones are Carlos Gomes and Heitor Villa-Lobos. Gomes (1836–1896) was a distinguished nineteenth-century romantic composer born in Campinas,

Brazil. He was one of the first New World composers to be accepted by the musical establishment in Europe. He became the protégé of D. Pedro II, Emperor of Brazil. He wrote piano pieces and operas, the most famous of which is *Il Guarany*, based on a romantic novel by the nineteenth-century Brazilian writer José de Alencar.

Villa-Lobos (1887–1959) is perhaps the most well-known South American classical composer. He was largely self-taught and wrote *Bachianas Brasileiras*, inspired by the art of Johann Sebastian Bach and the Brazilian musical tradition. He traveled extensively in Brazil collecting samples of folk songs, even going to the Amazon to familiarize himself with the music of the indigenous peoples. He wrote many piano pieces that incorporated both Brazilian folk music and stylistic elements of European tradition.

Culinary Expressions

There are many interesting culinary traditions in Brazil due to the diversity of immigrant populations. There are Italian, Japanese, Chinese, German, and many other immigrant groups that have contributed to the tastes and aromas of the Brazilian kitchen. But the national dish of Brazil comes from an unlikely source: concocted by African slaves, *feijoada* is based on pork leftovers and black beans. The white slave masters would throw away the pig's snout, feet, and ears. Slaves would assemble a heavy stew with pork pieces and fat in order to feed themselves. The wonderful smells coming from the kitchen would eventually entice a whole nation, and *feijoada* became a national standard. Nowadays you can be served *feijoada* in fancy, five-star hotels. Today, the snout and feet are usually replaced by generous pieces of pork sausage, but traditionalists still keep tasty pigs' ears in the mix.

If you're interested in trying to make this and other Brazilian dishes at home, go to your local bookstore and invest in a couple of Brazilian cookbooks. You can also find lots of great recipes online. One website that offers a recipe for *feijoada* is *www.brazilbrazil.com*.

What's on Brazilian TV?

Brazil is world famous for its *novelas* or television soap operas. Unlike American TV soaps, which can go on for decades, *novelas* normally last six to eight months at the most. Because the *novelas* are so popular, they have been exported to Portugal, where the Portuguese people have learned how to pronounce some typically Brazilian idioms. One of the most famous Brazilian soaps was *Roque Santeiro*, which had been banned during the military dictatorship for its irreverent humor and distinctly anti-government bias. It was later remade in the early nineties to great success. Because of its popularity, the writers even extended the *capítulos* or "daily episodes" to make the novela last longer. If you have extended cable or satellite TV service, you can watch current novelas on Brazilian channels, especially the *Globo* network, one of the biggest and most-watched channels in Brazil.

Brazilian Cinema

Brazil has made a significant contribution to international cinema, starting from the sixties revolution of modernist cinema *novo* with directors Glauber Rocha and Nelson Pereira dos Santos to the more recent work of Carlos Diegues, Hector Babenco, and Walter Salles. Here is a list of the titles, dates, and corresponding Brazilian directors.

AWARD-WINNING BRAZILIAN MOVIES		
TITLE	**YEAR**	**DIRECTOR**
Vidas Secas (Barren Lives)	1963	Glauber Rocha
Terra em Transe (Land in Torment)	1967	Glauber Rocha
Macunaíma (Jungle Freaks)	1969	Joaquim Pedro de Andrade
Bye Bye Brasil (Bye Bye Brazil)	1979	Carlos Diegues
Pixote, lei do mais fraco (Pixote)	1981	Hector Babenco
A Hora da Estrela (The Hour of the Star)	1985	Suzana Amaral
Terra Estrangeira (Foreign Land)	1995	Walter Salles/ Daniela Thomas
Central do Brasil (Central Station)	1998	Walter Salles

There are more recent examples of Brazilian cinema that include films such as *Cidade de Deus* (City of God) (2002) by directors Fernando Meirelles and Katia Lund, and *Madame Satā* (Madam Satā) (2002) by first-timer Karim Aïnouz. A new breed of filmmakers from the northeast has given Brazilian cinema a decidedly more gritty style. Two very recent examples of this *nordestino* ("northeastern") wave are *Amarelo Manga* (2002) by innovative director Cláudio Assis and *Árido Movie* (2004) by equally creative Lírio Ferreira. Find out more about Brazilian filmmakers at the following websites:

- *www.brazilbrazil.com/cinema*: The BrazilBrazil site is entirely dedicated to all things Brazilian, and includes a very good synopsis of Brazilian cinema.
- *www.curtaocurta.com.br*: A site dedicated to short films from Brazil with interesting links.
- *www.humnet.ucla.edu/spanport/faculty/randalj:* Randal Johnson, the UCLA professor who wrote Brazilian Cinema (Columbia UP, 1995) has a very informative page on Brazilian culture and cinema.

Where to Go?

Depending on where you travel in Brazil, there are several activities you will want to do and places you will want to visit. Brazil is a large, continental country, and the weather can be varied, depending if you are in the northeast or in the south. Here are some major cities to visit and activities to do while you are there. The chart on the next page is organized starting from the northernmost part of Brazil going south to the center-west region and back up north again to the Amazon. This list of cultural activities is very far from exhaustive, so be sure to contact the local tourism authority, dress appropriately, and most of all, enjoy the trip!

REGION	STATE	INTERESTING SITES
northeast	Maranhão	Capital City of São Luis
Activities: watch the Bumba-meu-Boi festival		
northeast	Ceará	Jericoacoara Beach
Activities: drive a buggy on the sandy dunes		
northeast	Rio Grande do Norte	Natal
Activities: visit a mangrove or cashew farm		
northeast	Pernambuco	Recife
Activities: dance with the Carnaval troupe Galo da Madrugada		
northeast	Pernambuco	Olinda
Activities: experience the stunning view from the Catedral de Sé located on Olinda's highest hill		
northeast	Bahia	Salvador
Activities: visit the Farol lighthouse; dance at the nearby clubs		
northeast	Bahia	Porto Seguro
Activities: visit the beach purported to be the site of the first Portuguese landing; enjoy restaurants with local flavors		
northeast	Alagoas	Maceió and surroundings
Activities: walk along hundreds of kilometers of white, sandy beaches		
southeast	Rio de Janeiro	Capital City of Rio
Activities: dance with the locals in an escola de samba; walk up to see the statue of Cristo Redentor on top of Corcovado Hill.		
southeast	São Paulo	Capital City of São Paulo
Activities: enjoy the finest European-style restaurants and nightclubs		
south	Rio Grande do Sul	Porto Alegre
Activities: visit a gaúcho restaurant and drink chimarrão, the strong Brazilian tea		
center-west	Minas Gerais	Ouro Preto
Activities: visit the beautiful gold-laden baroque churches and colonial cities		

REGION	STATE	INTERESTING SITES
center-west	Goiás	Brasília
Activities: visit the amazing modern architecture of the Brazilian capital		
center-west	Goiás	Pantanal
Activities: travel along the natural habitat of hundreds of species of the wetlands ecosystem named Pantanal		
north	Amazonas	Manaus
Activities: walk around the myriad of stands at the famous local market Ver-o-Peso		

In the next few sections we will present important information about some of the key Brazilian cities that make Brazil one of the most beautiful places in South America.

Brasília: The Modern Capital City

Located in the *centro-oeste* or the center-west region of Brazil, this modern capital was planned and constructed in the span of four years, from 1956 to 1960. It was largely the vision of then-President Juscelino Kubischek, who was able to take an idea that started in the nineteenth century and bring it to fruition.

One of the major modernist architects of Brasília was Oscar Niemeyer, who, along with Lúcio Costa's team, envisioned the large vertical structures of the *Palácio do Congresso* (National Congress), as well as the Cathedral of Brasília and many other stunning modernist buildings throughout the city. Below is a list of buildings that should be visited while you are in Brasília.

MODERNIST ARCHITECTURE OF BRASÍLIA	
PORTUGUESE	**ENGLISH**
Palácio do Congresso	National Congress
Palácio do Planalto	Executive Branch Offices
Palácio do Itamaraty	Foreign Relations or the Diplomatic Corps Office
Catedral de Brasília	Cathedral of Brasília
Palácio da Alvorada	Alvorada Palace (President's residence)
Esplanada dos Ministérios	Row of Ministries/Departments

The idea behind the city was to create a modern and functional plan that would also reflect the newer vision of a modern, democratic government. Some of the buildings are certainly that, and much more. The beauty of reflective pools, the accompanying sculptures, and the simple vertical and horizontal lines make a stunning city.

 Fact

Initially constructed to accommodate about 500,000 people, the city grew beyond its original plan and now has more than 2 million inhabitants, if one counts the so-called "satellite cities" that sprouted up at the very inception of the city.

Most people who live in Brasília enjoy living there, even if there are some typically urban problems. Public transportation can be inefficient, and one probably needs a car to get around the vast expanse of the *Planalto Central* (Central Plains). There might be very little to do on the weekends since it is a "working city" dedicated to the government bureaucracy. On the positive side, the weather is absolutely perfect, there is little pollution and virtually no threat from natural disasters, and the sunsets of the plains are absolutely gorgeous. So, if you visit Brazil, don't forget to stop by its most intriguing capital.

Rio de Janeiro and São Paulo: Big Metropoles

Both Rio and São Paulo are big cities and points of reference for traveling in Brazil. Several weekly flights from Chicago, New York, and Miami go directly to these Brazilian cities, both of which are situated in the southeastern region and are the two largest cities in the country and in South America.

Rio de Janeiro

Also known as *Cidade Maravilhosa* (Marvelous City), this urban center is marked by the incredible beauty of its surrounding hills and stunning beaches. The population of Rio is almost 6 million people, and up to 15 million if we count the total metropolitan area. Rio is a great cultural and economic center that boasts several important universities, such as the *Universidade Federal do Rio de Janeiro* or *UFRJ*, the *Universidade do Estado do Rio de Janeiro* or *UERJ*, and the *Pontifícia Universidade Católica do Rio de Janeiro* or *PUC-Rio*, which belongs to the great educational tradition of Catholic universities in Brazil.

One of the most famous images of Rio de Janeiro is of *Cristo Redentor* or "Christ the Redeemer," the art deco statue of Christ with open arms blessing the city. The Rio de Janeiro beaches attract tourists from around the world, and for native *cariocas* (the name given to those born in Rio) they are part of daily life. Beach culture is almost synonymous with Brazilian culture; it is no wonder that the "Brazilian bikini wax" first became popular among beachgoers in Copacabana, later expanding to California and now the entire world.

 **Essential**

Some of the most famous beaches of the world are found in Rio: the famous Ipanema and Copacabana beaches have been celebrated in songs heard around the world. The view of the Guanabara Bay is a natural postcard of Brazil, showing its unique view of mountains and beaches in close proximity.

One of the most important events in Brazilian culture is the annual *Carnaval* parade in Rio. Every February Brazilians watch hours of footage of dancing performers and intricately decorated floats that cross the *Sambódromo*, the name of the place constructed specifically for the parade.

One of the biggest events in Rio is also the end-of-the-year celebration when Brazilians bring in the New Year on the night of December 31st wearing traditional white and throwing flowers into the ocean, accompanied by intense fireworks and a party that lasts all night, aptly called the *Reveillón*, from the French word *reveiller* or "to wake up!"

São Paulo

The city of São Paulo has just about 10 million people (17 million if we count the larger metropolitan area). It is the second most populous city in Latin America, losing only to Mexico City. But it is the biggest city in South America, and indeed one of the largest in the world.

São Paulo has welcomed an incredibly diverse international population with immigrants from Italy, China, Japan, and Lebanon, to name a few. The Italian neighborhood of Bexiga in São Paulo is larger than the city of Naples. And the neighborhood of Liberdade, initially populated by Japanese immigrants, now has a large Asian population, with people from Korea and China, among other countries. In this neighborhood, children are taught to speak Asian languages. One of the best places to buy *sashimi* or to watch a folkloric dance show is in these streets of São Paulo. But new arrivals to São Paulo do not come only from overseas. A large population of people from the northeast of Brazil have significantly contributed to the construction, the economic wealth, and even the cultural makeup of the city.

This financial capital also accommodates the culturally savvy: São Paulo is home to the *Museu de Arte de São Paulo*, also known as the *MASP*, which runs internationally recognized exhibitions throughout the year. It has also a highly respected collection of modern art classics. The famous art exhibition called *Bienal de Artes* is a must-see for art lovers around the world.

São Paulo is also known for its passionate nightlife. Much like New York City, the city never sleeps, and the diversity of venues is truly breathtaking. But if dancing all night is not your cup of tea, São Paulo is home to a beautiful city park called *Ibirapuera* where family and friends gather every morning for a healthy jog or a bike ride.

The Northeast of Brazil: Culture and Tradition

This is one of the most sought-after tourist regions of Brazil. It makes up almost one-fifth of the country and its population is close to 45 million people. The northeast encompasses thousands of miles of white, sandy beaches and perfect tropical weather. The interior of the region is marked by almost untouched forests and more humid weather.

 Fact

The Portuguese explorer Pedro Álvares Cabral first landed in the region that is now called *Porto Seguro*, located in the northeastern state of Bahia, on April 22, 1500. But the colonization efforts by the Portuguese really started about fifty years later, with various excursions by the French and Dutch, who also settled in Brazil.

The intrinsic cultural, economic, and geographic variation of the region makes it difficult to talk about the northeast in general terms. Here are some historical and cultural highlights of the most interesting places to visit in the northeast.

The state of Pernambuco was one of the most prosperous *capitanías* or provinces of the colonial government, with record production of sugarcane in the seventeenth century. The *Quilombo dos Palmares* is the name given to a successful community of ex-slaves who escaped the hardships of working the sugarcane fields. Nowadays you can visit the *Museu do Homem do Nordeste* where you can appreciate historical items such as a collection of porcelain sugar bowls from that time period.

 Fact

The name *Pelourinho* comes from the Portuguese word for the "whipping post" where slaves were tied and punished. Nowadays the *Pelourinho* refers to several blocks of cobblestone streets in the hills of the city of Salvador where artists, musicians, and community activists have established themselves. A city within a city, the *Pelourinho* is where you will find restaurants with local Afro-Brazilian foods, dance studios, and many arts and crafts stores.

The state of Bahia carries many cultural traditions of Africans, with typical foods sold on the streets by *baianas* (women dressed in typical African garb) and *capoeira*, a type of martial arts that includes dance and music. The city of Salvador is famous for its colonial architecture and influential musical styles, especially in the *Pelourinho* district.

The state of Maranhão is known for its forests and mineral production, as well as for one of the most beautiful capital cities in the northeast. São Luis do Maranhão is the only state capital originally started by the French in the early seventeenth century. The name of the city is in honor of King Louis XII of France. The city was later taken over by the Dutch and eventually the Portuguese.

Recife, the capital city of Pernambuco, is also known as the "Brazilian Venice" because it was built in between two rivers, the Capibaribe and the Beberibe Rivers, and its many bridges resemble the Italian city. It is also one of the largest cities in the northeast (with a population of about 1.5 million people) and a well-known cultural center.

Just north of Recife there is the city of Olinda, a beautiful town of colonial architecture that has been designated as a World Heritage Site by UNESCO in 1982 due to the preservation of its original colonial buildings. During *Carnaval*, many revelers parade on its old streets dancing the *frevo* and the *maracatu*.

Fortaleza, the capital city of the state of Ceará, has one of the liveliest beach-front nightlives of the northeast region. The *Praia de Iracema* or Iracema Beach is famous for its warm waters.

The northeast region has one of the most interesting arts-and-crafts traditions of the country. Some of the most beautiful handmade clothing can be found in many northeastern markets. As you plan your vacation to Brazil, do not hesitate to visit at least one of these northeastern states. If you are interested in water sports, colonial architecture, or simply relaxing at the beach without big crowds, the northeast is for you!

Florianópolis and Other Southern Belles

The south of Brazil also has its charm. One of the most beautiful sites in the south of Brazil is the city of Florianópolis, charmingly referred to by its inhabitants as Floripa. The city is the capital of Santa Catarina and is located on an island surrounded by other smaller islets. It has a population of a bit more than 800,000 inhabitants and a beauty of its own.

The city was originally settled by Azorean Portuguese, but the influence of Germans and Italians is clearly seen by the architecture and the presence of immigrant communities.

One of the largest and most important cities in the south of Brazil is Curitiba, with more than 1.5 million people living in the larger metropolitan area. In this city, you will be able to enjoy one of the most efficient and environmentally friendly transportation systems in Latin America. Buses stop near clear, elevated tubes where people get in once and can ride for the entire day. The city is also one of the "greenest" in Brazil, with well-kept parks.

The city of Porto Alegre is one of the largest cities of the south, and the closest big city to the South American countries of Argentina, Uruguay, Paraguay, and Chile. It is a large urban, industrialized center that is important to the *Mercosul*, the Brazilian version of the NAFTA. Business people from South America often stop first in Porto Alegre to conduct business and trade with Brazilians. Porto Alegre is the capital of Rio Grande do Sul and the home of the *gaúcho*, or Brazilian cowboy, culture. There you can also find many *churrascarias* or restaurants that serve the typical Brazilian barbecue, a never-ending feast of different meats that are brought to the table on long spears. These types of restaurants are becoming increasingly popular in big American cities such as Miami, Boston, New York, and Los Angeles.

More to the south of Porto Alegre you will find the small city of Gramado, located in the hills of the Serra Gaúcha, an area heavily influenced by the German settlers. Gramado is home to the Gramado Film Festival, one of the most influential festivals of avant-garde films in South America. An interesting mix of Brazilian and European culture can be found in these "Southern Belles."

This book is only a small window into the vast world of Brazilian Portuguese. In it, you have found but a taste of the variety of vocabulary, expressions, and newly formed words in this language. If you wish to continue learning more phrases in Brazilian Portuguese, make sure to search the Internet using phrases such as *português brasileiro* (pohr-too-GHE-ees brah-zee-LEY-roo) or Brazilian Portuguese. Enjoy your travels to Brazil!

APPENDIX A
ENGLISH TO PORTUGUESE GLOSSARY

a lot
muito

abdominal
abdominal

able
capaz

absolutely not!
absolutamente!

abstinence
abstinência

acceptable
aceitável

accessible
acessível

accident
acidente

accommodating
acomodável

accountant
contador,
contadora

achieve, to
conseguir

action
ação

actor
ator

actress
atriz

acute accent
acento agudo

address
endereço

admissible
admissível

adolescence
adolescência

adorable
adorável

affable
afável

affection
carinho

against
contra

airplane
avião

all
todos, todas

all, entire
todo, toda

allow, to
permitir

already
já

also
também

always
sempre

American
americano,
americana

anaconda
sucuri

and
e

angel
anjo

Angola
Angola

Angolan
angolano,
angolana

animal
animal

annex
anexo

anniversary
aniversário

annual
anual

answer the
phone, to
atender o
telefone

answer, to
responder

anwering
machine
secretária
(eletrônica)

anxious
ansioso, ansiosa

any
qualquer

applaud, to
aplaudir

apple
maçã

approve, to
passar

April
abril

apron
avental

architect
arquiteto,
arquiteta

ardor
ardor

area code
código de área

Argentina
Argentina

Argentinian
argentino,
argentina

armadillo
tatu

aroused
excitado,
excitada

arrest, to
prender

arrive, to
chegar

arrive, to
vir

art
arte

artist
artista

as much as
tanto... quanto

as . . . as
tão . . . quanto

ask for, to
pedir

asleep
dormindo

astral
astral

at the same time
ao mesmo tempo

atheist
ateu, atéia

athlete
atleta

athleticism
atletismo

attack
ataque

attend, to
assistir (a)

attention
atenção

attentively, cordially
atenciosamente

auditor
auditor

August
agosto

aunt
tia

Australia
Austrália

Australian
australiano, australiana

Austria
Áustria

Austrian
austríaco, austríaca

author
autor

automobile
automóvel

autumn, fall
outono

average height
estatura mediana

avoidable
evitável

awake
acordado, acordada

backpack
mochila

bad
ruim

bag
bolsa

baggage
bagagem

bakery
padaria

bald
careca

bank
banco

bank teller
bancário

barbershop
barbeiro

basketball
basquetebol

bath
banho

be (situated), to
ficar

be able to, to
poder

be afraid, to
ter medo

be surprised, to
surpreender-se com

be windy, to
ventar

be, to
estar, ser

beans
feijão

beautiful
lindo, linda

beauty salon
salão de beleza

because
porque

become, to
ficar

beef
carne de boi

beer
cerveja

before
antes

behind
atrás, detrás de

Belgian
belga

Belgium
Bélgica

believe, to
acreditar

belt
cinto

better
melhor

big
grande

bill, account
conta

billfold
carteira

billion
bilhão

biodegradable
biodegradável

bird
pássaro

birthday
aniversário

black pepper
pimenta do reino

blasphemous
blasfemável

blind
cego

blond
louro, loura

blouse
blusa

blue
azul

board
quadro

boat, ship
nau, navio

bonbon
bombom

book
livro

bookstore
livraria

boring
chato, chata

both
ambos, ambas

bowsprit
proa

boy
menino

boyfriend
namorado

Brazil
Brasil

Brazilian
brasileiro,
brasileira

bread
pão

brevity
brevidade

bride
noiva

bring, to
trazer

British
britânico,
britânica

brother
irmão

brother-in-law
cunhado

brown
marrom

brush/comb
(oneself), to
pentear-se

building
prédio

business
partner
sócio, social

busy
ocupado,
ocupada

but, however
porém

butcher shop
açougue

buy, to
comprar, fazer
compras

bye
tchau

cake
bolo

calculating
calculável

call oneself, to
chamar-se

call, to
chamar, ligar

call (someone
or something
a name), to
chamar de

calm
tranqüilo,
tranqüila

Canada
Canadá

Canadian
canadense

capital
capital

captain
capitão

car
carro

cardiac
cardíaco

cards
cartões

care
cuidado

careful
(exclamation)
cuidado

cashew fruit
caju

cat
gato

catch, to
pegar

cathedral
catedral

celebrated
comemorado,
comemorada

celebrity
pessoa famosa

censor
censor

center
centro

central
central

central-west
centro-oeste

chaos
caos

chapter
capítulo

cheap
barato, barata

cheese
queijo

chess
xadrez

chest
baú

child
criança

Chile
Chile

Chilean
chileno, chilena

China
China

Chinese
chinês, chinesa

chocolate
chocolate

choose, to
escolher

Christmas
Dia de Natal

church
igreja

circumflex
accent
acento
circunflexo

city
cidade

clarinet
clarinete

clarity
claridade

class
aula

classroom
sala de aula

clean
limpo, limpa

clearly
claramente

client
consumidor

climax
clímax

clinic
clínica

close, nearby
perto

clothes designer
*costureiro,
costureira*

clothing store
loja de roupa

cloudy
nublado

club, gym
clube

coat
casaco

code
código, senha

coffee
café

cold
frio

cold cuts
frios

collect call
*chamada
a cobrar*

Colombia
Colombia

Colombian
*colombiano,
colombiana*

color
cor

comb
pente

come back, to
voltar

come, arrived
vindo

come, to
vir

comedian
comediante

comedy
comédia

comfortable
confortável

commercial
comercial

communi-
cate, to
comunicar

communication
comunicação

compete, to
competir

competitors
concorrentes

complain
about, to
queixar-se de

complete, to
completar

complex
complexo

compose, to
compor

composer
compositor

comprehend, to
compreender

comprehensible
compreensível

computer
computador

concert
concerto

conductor
condutor

conference
conferência

congested
(by a cold)
constipado

conspirer
conspirador

consulate
consulado

consultant
*consultor,
consultora*

consumed
*consumido,
consumida*

consumer
consumidor

contruct, to
construir

conversation
(colloquial)
bate-papo

convertible
conversível

convince one-
self of, to
convencer-se de

cordial
cordial

cordially
*saudações
cordiais*

cordless phone
telefone sem fio

corner
esquina

correct
certo

correct, to
corrigir

Costa Rica
Costa Rica

Costa Rican
costa-riquenho

cotton
algodão

counting
contagem

country code
*código
internacional*

couple
casal

cousin (female)
prima

cousin (male)
primo

covered
coberto

cradle
berço

crazy
louco, louca

creature
criatura

credit
crédito

crime
crime, delito

cruel
cruel

Cuba
Cuba

cultural
cultural

culture
cultura

cup
xícara

curable
curável

curious
curioso

currency exchange agency
casa de câmbio

customer
freguês, freguesa

customs
alfândega

cycle, ring
ciclo

cyclist
ciclista

Czech
checo, checa

Czech Republic
República Checa

dad, daddy
papai

dance, to
dançar

dark-skinned
moreno, morena

daughter
filha

daughter-in-law
nora

day
dia

day after tomorrow
depois de amanhã

day before yesterday
anteontem

dear (formal)
prezado, prezada

dear (informal)
caro, cara, querido, querida

December
dezembro

decide to, to
decidir-se a

dedicate (oneself to), to
dedicar-se a

demand, to
exigir

dentist
dentista

desire, to
desejar

destroyer
destruidor

detector
detetor

development
desenvolvimento

dial tone
sinal

dice
dado

dictionary
dicionário

died, dead
morto

dieresis
trema

difficult
difícil

digestable
digestível

direct call
ligação direta

director
diretor, diretora

dish
prato

divided
dividido

divorced
divorciado, divorciada

do, to
fazer

doctor
médico

document
documento

dog
cachorro, cão (male); cachorra, cadela (female)

dollars
dólares

domino
dominó

door
porta

dream
sonho

dress (oneself), to
vestir-se

dressmaker
costureiro, costureira

drink coffee, to
tomar café

drink, to
beber, tomar

drop
gota

drug, drugs
droga

drugstore
drogaria, farmácia

drunk
bêbado, bêbada

dry-cleaners
lava a seco

duck
pato

durable
durável

Dutch
*holandês,
holandesa*

dynasty
dinastia

early
cedo

earth, land
terra

easy
fácil

eat, to
comer

economic
*econômico,
econômica*

Ecuador
Ecuador

Ecuadorian
*equatoriano,
equatoriana*

editor
editor

educational
educacional

egg
ovo

Egypt
Egito

Egyptian
egípcio, egípcia

eight
oito

eight hundred
*oitocentos,
oitocentas*

eighteen
dezoito

eighth
oitavo, oitava

eighty
oitenta

elderly
idoso, idosa

electric guitar
guitarra

electronic
*eletrônico,
electrônica*

elegance
elegância

elegant
elegante

**elementary
school**
escola primária

elephant
elefante

eleven
onze

eleventh
*décimo-
primeiro,
décima-primeira*

embarassed
*envergonhado,
envergonhada*

embassy
embaixada

emotional
emocional

employee, maid
*empregado,
empregada*

engineer
*engenheiro,
engenheira*

England
Inglaterra

English
inglês, inglesa

enjoy, to
aproveitar

enjoy, to (slang)
curtir

enter, to
entrar em

**entertain
(oneself), to**
divertir-se

envelope
envelope

error, mistake
erro

escape
fuga

essay, rehearsal
ensaio

essential
*essencial,
imprescindível*

Europe
Europa

ever, never
jamais

exam
exame

excellent
excelente

exceptional
excepcional

excited
*animado,
animada*

exclude, to
excluir

**excuse me,
sorry**
com licença

exercise, to
fazer exercícios

exist, to
haver

exotic
exótico

expensive
caro

explain, to
explicar

explainable
explicável

explanations
explicações

eyeglasses
óculos

**facing, in
front of**
defronte de

factory worker
*operário,
operária*

falsifiable
falsificável

familiar, pertaining to family
familiar

family
família

famous
famoso, famosa

far from
longe de

fast
rápido, rápida

fat
gordo, gorda

fatal
fatal

father
pai

father-in-law
sogro

favor
favor

feat
façanha

February
fevereiro

federal
federal

fervor
fervor

few
poucos, poucas

fiancé
noivo

fiancée
noiva

fifteen
quinze

fifth
quinto, quinta

fifty
cinqüenta

find
arrumar

find, to
encontrar

find, to
achar

find (oneself), to
encontrar-se

finish, to
acabar, terminar

first
primeiro, primeira

five
cinco

five hundred
quinhentos, quinhentas

fix
arrumar

fluently
fluentemente

fly (insect)
mosca

fog
neblina

food
comida

forget to, to
esquecer-se de

fork
garfo

forklift
grúa

fortunately
felizmente

forty
quarenta

fossil
fóssil

four
quatro

four hundred
quatrocentos, quatrocentas

fourteen
catorze

fourth
quarto, quarta

France
França

French
francês, francesa

frequency
freqüência

Friday
sexta-feira

friend, partner
companheiro, companheira

frog
sapo

fundamental
fundamental

funny
engraçado, engraçada

future, future tense
futuro

garage
garagem

garlic cloves
dente de alho

German
alemão, alemã

Germany
Alemanha

gesture
gesto

get married, to
casar-se

get together, to
reunir-se

get used to, to
acostumar-se com

get, to
conseguir

gift
presente

girl
menina

girlfriend
namorada

give, to
dar

go on a short trip, to
dar uma volta

go on strike, to
fazer greve

go out (leave), to
sair

go to bed, to
deitar-se

go up, to
subir

go, to
ir

god
deus

goddaughter
afilhada

godfather
padrinho

godmother
madrinha

godson
afilhado

going-away party
festa de despedida

good
bom, boa

good afternoon
boa tarde

good evening
boa noite

good luck
boa sorte

good morning
bom dia

grammar
gramática

granddaughter
neta

grandfather
avô

grandma, granny
vovó

grandmother
avó

grandpa
vovô

grandson
neto

grave accent
acento grave

great
ótima

Great Britain
Grã-bretanha

great-grandfather
bisavô

great-grandmother
bisavó

Greece
Grécia

Greek
grego, grega

groom
noivo

guide
guia

gym
ginásio

hairdresser
cabelereiro

Haiti
Haiti

Haitian
haitiano, haitiana

ham
presunto

handed, given
entregue

handset
gancho

hang up the phone, to
desligar o telefone

hangover
ressaca

happiness
felicidade

happy
contente, feliz

have a good trip
boa viagem

have breakfast, to
tomar café

have dinner, to
jantar

have fun, to
divertir-se

have lunch, to
almoçar

have, to
ter

to have a dial tone
dar sinal

he
ele

hear, to
escutar, ouvir

heart
coração

Hebrew
hebreu, hebréia

hello
alô

help
socorro

help, to
ajudar

her (possessive)
dela

here
aqui

hey!
opa!

hi
oi, olá

himself/herself
si

his (possessive)
dele

Hindu
hindu

Holland
Holanda

homework
dever de casa

horrible
horrível

hospital
hospital

hot
calor

hot pepper sauce
pimenta malagueta

hotel
hotel

hour
hora

house
casa

how many
quantos, quantas

how much
quanto, quanta

hug
abraço

humid
húmido, húmida

humor
humor

hunt
caça

hurt (oneself), to
machucar-se

husband
marido

I
eu

idea
idéia

ideal
ideal

idealism
idealismo

identical
idêntico

identification tag
crachá

identity
identidade

illegal
ilegal

image
imagem

immediately
imediatamente

impede, to
impedir

importance
importância

important
importante

impose, to
impor

impossible
impossível

impressed
impressionado, impressionada

in
em

in front of
em frente de

in love
apaixonado, apaixonada

include, to
incluir

included
incluído, incluída

incomparable
incomparável

Independence Day
Dia da Independência

India
India

Indian
indiano, indiana

indoor soccer
futebol de salão

inevitable
inevitável

inferior
inferior

inform, to
informar

information
informação

inside
dentro de

insistence
insistência

inspector
inspetor

instructor
instrutor

intelligent
inteligente

international
internacional

Internet café
cyber café

introduce, to
apresentar

invent, to
inventar

inventor
inventor

invest, to
investir

Iran
Irã

Iranian
iraniano, iraniana

Iraq
Iraque

Iraqi
iraquiano, iraquiana

Ireland
Irlanda

Irish
irlandês, irlandesa

irritated
irritado, irritada

Israel
Israel

Israeli
israelense

Italian
italiano, italiana

Italy
Itália

Jamaica
Jamaica

Jamaican
jamaicano, jamaicana

January
janeiro

Japan
Japão

Japanese
japonês, japonesa

jealousy
ciúme

judge
juiz, juíza

July
julho

June
junho

kennel
canil

key
chave

king
rei

kiss
beijo

kiss (one another), to
beijar-se

knife
faca

know (information, skills), to
saber

know (people, places), to
conhecer

lack, to
fazer falta

lamentable
lamentável

last week
na semana passada

late
tarde

Latin America
América Latina

laugh, to
rir

laugh (at), to
rir-se de

lawyer
advogado, advogada

learn, to
aprender

leave a message, to
deixar um recado

leave, to
deixar

leave, to
partir

legume
legume

less
menos

lesson
lição

liberty
liberdade

library
biblioteca

lie, to
mentir

lightening
relâmpago

like, to
gostar de

likewise, same here
igualmente

liqueur
licor

Lisbon
Lisboa

listen, to
escutar, ouvir

live, to
viver

live, to (reside)
morar

local
local

long distance
interurbano

look like, to
parecer-se com

look (at oneself), to
olhar-se

look (at), to
olhar para

lose, to
perder

lotion
loção

love
amor

love, to
amar

baggage, luggage
bagagem

ma'am, lady
senhora

macaw
arara

made, done
feito

make, to
fazer

magazines
revistas

make a phone call, to
fazer um telefonema

make peace, to
fazer as pazes

mall
shopping

manager
gerente

map
mapa

March
março

married
casado, casada

match
fósforo

May
maio

may
poder

May I help you?
Pois não?

mechanic
mecânico

medicine, medication
medicina, remédios

melon
melão

mentor
mentor

Merry Christmas
Feliz Natal

message
recado

Mexican
mexicano,
mexicana

Mexico
México

midnight
meia-noite

milk
leite

million
milhão

millionaire
milionário

minus
menos

mirror
espelho

miserable
miserável

miss, to
fazer falta

mister, sir
senhor

modern
moderno,
moderna

mom, mommy
mamãe

moment
momento

Monday
segunda-feira

money
dinheiro

more
mais

mother
mãe

mother-in-law
sogra

motor, engine
motor

movie
filme

movies, cinema
cinema

Mozambique
Moçambique

multiple choice
múltipla escolha

museum
museu

music
música

musician
músico, música

my
meu, minha
(plural: meus,
minhas)

naked
nu, nua

name
nome

nap
cochilo

napkin
guardanapo

national
nacional

natural
natural

nature
natureza

necklace
corrente, colar

need, to
precisar de

negotiable
negociável

neighbor
vizinho, vizinha

neighborhood
bairro

neither
também não

neither . . . nor
nem . . . nem

nephew
sobrinho

nervous
nervoso,
nervosa

never
nunca

new
novo, nova

newspaper
jornal

newspaper
seller
jornaleiro

newsstand
banca de revista

Nicaragua
Nicarágua

Nicaraguan
nicaragüense

nice
simpático

nice to
meet you
encantado,
encantada

nice to
meet you
muito prazer

niece
sobrinha

nine
nove

nine hundred
novecentos,
novecentas

nineteen
dezenove

ninety
noventa

ninth
nono, nona

no
não

nobody
ninguém

noise
barulho

noon, midday
meio-dia

normal
normal

north
norte

North America
América do
Norte

northeast
nordeste

not one
*nenhum,
nenhuma*

not yet
ainda não

notebook
caderno

nothing
nada

November
novembro

number
número

obvious
óbvio

October
outubro

office
escritório

official
oficial

official meeting
audiência

old
velho, velha

on top
em cima de

one
um, uma

**one hundred
and one**
cento e um, uma

onion
cebola

open, to
abrir

opened
aberto

**operator, direc-
tory assistance**
*telefonista,
ajuda ao
assinante*

opposing
opositor

orange
laranja

organ
órgão

organizable
organizável

original
original

orphan
órfão

ostensible
ostensível

other
outro, outra

our
nosso, nossa

outside
fora

over, on top
sobre

overcome, to
passar

page
página

paid
pago

pain
dor

paintbrush
pincel

pale
pálido, pálida

Panama
Panamá

Panamenian
*panamenho,
panamenha*

paper
papel

paper
trabalho

pardon, sorry
perdão

park
parque

partial
parcial

party
festa

pass, to
passar

passable
passável

past
*passado,
passada*

pastor
pastor

patience
paciência

pay, to
pagar

peach
pêssego

pediatrician
pediatra

pen
caneta

pencil
lápis

people
gente

perfume
perfume

persistent
persistente

**personal
infinitive**
infinitivo pessoal

pharmacist
*farmacêutico,
farmacêutica*

phenomenal
fenomenal

Philippines
Filipinas

phone book
*catálogo
telefônico*

phone card
*cartão
telefônico*

phone number
*número de
telefone*

photographer
*fotógrafo,
fotógrafa*

phrase
frase

physical
físico

physicist
físico

pianist
pianista

pig's ear
orelha de porco

pig's foot
pé de porco

pig's tail
rabo de porco

pilot
piloto

pineapple
abacaxi

piranha
piranha

pity
dó

place
lugar

place, to
colocar, pôr

plane, leveled
plano

planet
planeta

play (a sport or game), to
jogar

play (an instrument), to
tocar

please
por favor

please (formal)
por gentileza, por obséquio

pleasure
prazer

Poland
Polônia

police
polícia

policeman
guarda

Polish
polonês, polonesa

poor
pobre

popular
popular

populated
populoso, populosa

pork
carne de porco

Portugal
Portugal

possible
possível

postcard
cartão postal

poster
cartaz

potent
potente

power
potência

presentable
presentável

president
presidente

press, to
apertare

pretend, to
fazer de conta

preterite tense
pretérito

pretty
bonito, bonita

problem
problema

profession
profissão

program
programa

progressive present
presente contínuo

proposal
proposta

protector
protetor

psychotherapist
analista

pub
barzinho

purple
roxo

purse
bolsa

put in jail
pôr na cadeia

put, set
posto

put, to
colocar, pôr

question
pergunta

radio
rádio

rain, to
chover

ranking
ranking

rational
racional

raw
cru, crua

react, to
reagir

read, to
ler

receive, to
receber

recognized
reconhecido, reconhecida

red
vermelho, vermelha

redhead, redheaded
ruivo, ruiva

reflect, to
refletir

reflector, reflecting
refletor

remember, to
recordar

remember to, to
lembrar-se

remembrance, souvenir
lembrança

reporter, journalist
jornalista

reptile
réptil

Republican
republicano, republicana

respectable
respeitável

rest, to
descansar

restaurant
restaurante

rested
*descansado,
descansada*

retire, to
deitar-se

rice
arroz

rich
rico, rica

ride a bike, to
*andar de
bicicleta*

rifle
fuzil

right, indeed
pois é

river
rio

root
raiz

rumor
rumor

run, to
correr

sad
triste

said
dito

saint
santo

Saint Patrick's Day
*Dia de São
Patrício*

salesperson
*vendedor,
vendedora*

salt
sal

same
mesmo

sandwich
sanduíche

satisfied
*satisfeito,
satisfeita*

Saturday
sábado

say (imperative)
diga

say, to
dizer

scared
*amedrontado,
amendrontada*

scheme, plan
*esquema,
complô*

school
escola

sea, ocean
mar

second
*segundo,
segunda*

secretary
secretária

section
seção

seductor
sedutor

see, to
ver

see you later
até mais

see you soon
*até breve,
até logo*

see you tomorrow
até amanhã

seen
visto

sell, to
vender

sensational
sensacional

separated
*separado,
separada*

September
setembro

serious
sério, séria

serve, to
servir

service
atendimento

set, to
pôr

seven
sete

seven hundred
*setecentos,
setecentas*

seventeen
dezessete

seventh
sétimo, sétima

seventy
setenta

shave, to
fazer a barba

she
ela

shoe store
*sapataria, loja
de sapatos*

short
baixo, baixa

sick
doente

sick, bored, boring
*enjoado,
enjoada*

simple
simples

since
desde

sing, to
cantar

singer
cantor, cantora

single
solteiro, solteira

sinister
sinistro

sister
irmã

sister-in-law
cunhada

sit, to
sentar-se

situation
situação

six
seis

six hundred
seiscentos, seiscentas

sixteen
dezesseis

sixth
sexto, sexta

sixty
sessenta

size
tamanho

sky
céu

slave quarters
senzala

sleep, to
dormir

slowly
devagar

snow
neve

snow, to
nevar

so
assim

so many
tantos, tantas

so much
tanto, tanta

sober
sóbrio, sóbria

soccer
futebol

socialist
socialista

sofa
sofá

some, something
algum, alguma

someone
alguém

son
filho

song
música

song
canção

son-in-law
genro

sorry
desculpe, desculpa

so-so
mais ou menos

soup
sopa

south
sul

South America
América do Sul

southeast
sudeste

speak, to
falar

specialist
especialista

speech, language
fala

spend, to
gastar

sport
esporte

spouse
esposo, esposa

spring
primavera

stairs
escadas

start, to
começar

state
estado

statement
afirmação

stationary store
papelaria

stay, to
ficar

stepfather
padrasto

stepmother
madrasta

storage facility
armazém

store
loja

street
rua

street market
feira

street vendor
vendedor, vendedora ambulante

strong, stocky
forte

student
estudante

student center
centro estudantil

studious
estudioso, estudiosa

study, to
estudar

stunned
estupefato, estupefata

stupid
burro, burra

such
tal

suddenly, all of sudden
de repente

sugarcane rum
cachaça

summer
verão

sun, sunny
sol

Sunday
domingo

superior
superior

supermarket
supermercado

Sure!, Of course!
Pois não!

surprising
surpreendente

Sweden
Suécia

Swedish
sueco, sueca

sweet
doce

Swiss
suíço, suíça

Switzerland
Suíça

systems analyst
analista de sistemas

table
mesa

take advantage of, to
aproveitar

take, to
tirar

talent
talento

talk (n.), conversation
conversa

tall
alto, alta

task, homework
tarefa

taxi
táxi

tea
chá

teacher, professor
professor, professora

telephone
telefone

telephone booth
orelhão

telephone call
telefonema

telephone set
aparelho (telefônico)

television
televisão

ten
dez

tennis player
tenista

tenor
tenor

tenth
décimo, décimo

test
prova

Thai
tailandês, tailandesa

Thailand
Tailândia

thank you
obrigado, obrigada

that
aquele, aquela

that (neutral, abstract)
aquilo

the
o, a, os, as

theirs
deles, delas

then
então

then, that
que

there, over there
lá

these
esses, essas

they, them
eles, elas

thin
magro, magra

think
achar

think, to
refletir

third
terceiro, terceira

thirteen
treze

thirty
trinta

this
esse, essa, este, esta

this (neutral, abstract)
isso

thorax
tórax

those
aqueles, aquelas

thousand
mil

three
três

three hundred
trezentos, trezentas

thunder
trovoada

Thursday
quinta-feira

tilde
til

time, climate
tempo

times (occasions)
vezes

tired
cansado, cansada

title
título

to
para

to you, him, her (indirect pronoun)
lhe

today
hoje

together
juntos, juntas

tomorrow
amanhã

too much
demais

touch, to
tocar

traditional
tradicional

traffic
trânsito

train
trem

transfer
transferência

transfer, to
transferir

trash
lixo

travel, to
viajar

traveler's checks
cheques de viagem

tree
árvore

trip
viagem

truck
caminhão

truth
verdade

Tuesday
terça-feira

turkey
peru

twelfth
décimo-segundo, décima-segunda

twelve
doze

twentieth
vigésimo, vigésima

twenty
vinte

twenty-one
vinte e um, vinte e uma

twenty-three
vinte e três

twenty-two
vinte e dois, vinte e duas

two
dois, duas

two hundred
duzentos, duzentas

type
tipo

ugly
feio, feia

uncle
tio

under
debaixo de, embaixo de

understand, to
entender

understand, to
compreender

usual
usual

vacation
ferias

Valentine's Day
Dia dos Namorados

valor
valor

value
valor

vegetable oil
óleo

vegetables
verduras

Venezuela
Venezuela

Venezuelan
venezuelano, venezuelana

very
muito

vinegar
vinagre

virgin
virgem

visit, to
visitar

voluntary, volunteer
voluntário

wait on, to
atender

waiter
garçom

waitress
garçonete

walk, to
andar

want, to
querer

war
guerra

wash, to
lavar

wash (oneself), to
lavar-se

watch, to
assistir (a)

way
jeito

we
nós

we (the people)
a gente

weak
fraco, fraca

weather
clima, tempo

Wednesday
quarta-feira

week
semana

weekend
fim de semana

welcome
bem-vindo, bem-vinda

well
bem

what, which
qual

what
que

when
quando

where
onde

where to, to where
aonde

while
enquanto

white
branco

who
quem

why
por quê

widow
viúva

widower
viúvo

wife, spouse
mulher

will
vontade

window
janela

wine
vinho

winter
inverno

wish, to
desejar

with
com

with credit card
*com cartão
de crédito*

with you (pl.)
(archaic)
convosco

won
ganho

wonder
maravilha

wonderful
*maravilhoso,
maravilhosa*

wood
pau

work
trabalho

work, to
trabalhar

worried
*preocupado,
preocupada*

worry about, to
*preocupar-
se com*

worse, the
worst
pior

Wow!
Nossa!

write, to
escrever

written
escrito

year
ano

yellow
*amarelo,
amarela*

yes
sim

yesterday
ontem

yet
ainda

you
tu, você, vocês

you (pl.)
(archaic)
vós

young
jovem

young boy
(pejorative)
moleque

young man
rapaz

youngest
offspring
caçula

youngster
jovem

your (familiar)
*teu, tua,
teus, tuas*

your (formal)
*seu, sua,
seus, suas*

yours (archaic)
vosso

zinc
zinco

Zulu
zulu

APPENDIX B
PORTUGUESE TO ENGLISH GLOSSARY

a, as
the (fem.)

a gente
we (the people)

abacaxi
pineapple

abdominal
abdominal

aberto
opened

abraço
hug

abril
April

abrir
to open

absolutamente!
absolutely not!

abstinência
abstinence

acabar
to finish

açaí
acai fruit, a wild berry found in the Amazon

ação
action

acessível
accessible

aceitável
acceptable

acento agudo
acute accent

acento circunflexo
circumflex accent

acento grave
grave accent

achar
to find, to think

acidente
accident

acomodável
accommodating

acordado, acordada
awake

Açores
also called the Azores, an archipelago or group of islands that belongs to Portugal

acostumar-se com
to get used to

açougue
butcher shop

acreditar
to believe

admissível
admissible

adolescência
adolescence, teenage years

adorável
adorable

advogado, advogada
lawyer

afável
affable

afilhada
goddaughter

afilhado
godson

afirmação
statement

agogô
two bells together, struck with a stick or squeezed together

agosto
August

ainda
yet

ainda não
not yet

ajudar
to help

Alemanha
Germany

alemão, alemã
German

alfândega
customs

algodão
cotton

alguém
someone

algum, alguma
some, something

almoçar
to have lunch

alô
hello

alto, alta
tall

amanhã
tomorrow

amar
to love

amarelo, amarela
yellow

Amazonas
a state in the north of Brazil

ambos, ambas
both

amendrontado, amendrontada
scared

América do Norte
North America

América do Sul
South America

América Latina
Latin America

americano, americana
American

amor
love

analista
psychotherapist

analista de sistemas
systems analyst

andar
to walk

andar de bicicleta
to ride a bike

anexo
annex

Angola
Angola

angolano, angolana
Angolan

animado, animada
excited

animal
animal

aniversário
birthday, anniversary

anjo
angel

ano
year

ansioso, ansiosa
anxious

anteontem
day before yesterday

antes
before

anual
annual

ao mesmo tempo
at the same time

aonde
where to, to where

apaixonado, apaixonada
in love

aparelho (telefônico)
telephone set

apertare
to press

aplaudir
to applaud

aprender
to learn

apresentar
to introduce

aproveitar
to take advantage of, to enjoy

aquele, aquela
that

aqueles, aquelas
those

aqui
here

aquilo
that (neutral, abstract)

arara
macaw

ardor
ardor

Argentina
Argentina

argentino, argentina
Argentinian

armazém
storage facility

arquiteto, arquiteta
architect

arroz
rice

arrumar
fix, find

arte
art

artista
artist

árvore
tree

às
to the (a + as contraction)

assim
so

assistir (a)
to attend, to watch

astral
astral

ataque
attack

até amanhã
see you tomorrow

até breve
see you soon

até logo
see you soon

até mais
see you later

atenção
attention

atenciosamente
attentively, cordially

atender
to answer the phone, to wait on

atender o telefone
to answer the phone

atendimento
service

ateu, atéia
atheist

atleta
athlete

atletismo
athleticism

ator
actor

atriz
actress

atrás
behind

audiência
official meeting

auditor
auditor

aula
class

Austrália
Australia

australiano, australiana
Australian

Áustria
Austria

austríaco, austríaca
Austrian

automóvel
automobile

autor
author

avental
apron

avião
airplane

avó
grandmother

avô
grandfather

azul
blue

bagagem
baggage, luggage

bairro
neighborhood

baixo, baixa
short

bambuzal
plantation of bamboo trees

banca de revista
newsstand

bancário
bank teller

banco
bank

Banco Central
Central Bank (the equivalent of the Federal Reserve)

banho
bath

barato, barata
cheap

barbeiro
barbershop

barulho
noise

barzinho
local pub

basquetebol
basketball

bate-papo
conversation, friendly chat (colloquial)

baú
chest

bêbado, bêbada
drunk

beber
to drink

beijar-se
to kiss one another

beijo
kiss

belga
Belgian

Bélgica
Belgium

bem
well

bem-vindo, bem-vinda
welcome

berço
cradle

berimbau
one-string African instrument

biblioteca
library

bilhão
one billion

biodegradável
biodegradable

bisavó
great-grandmother

bisavô
great-grandfather

blasfemável
blasphemous

blusa
blouse

boa noite
good evening

boa sorte
good luck

boa tarde
good afternoon

boa viagem
have a good trip

bolo
cake

bolsa
bag, purse

bom
good

bom dia
good morning

bombom
bonbon

bonito, bonita
pretty

Boniwa
indigenous language of Brazil

bonzinho, boazinha
very nice (about a person)

bossa nova
jazzy musical style that originated in the sixties in Brazil

branco
white

Brasil
Brazil

brasileiro, brasileira
Brazilian

brevidade
brevity

britânico, britânica
British

burro, burra
stupid

Caatinga
desert-like region of northeast Brazil

cabelereiro
hairdresser

caça
hunt

cachaça
sugarcane rum

cachorra
female dog

cachorro
dog

caçula
youngest offspring

caderno
notebook

café
coffee

caipirinha
a Brazilian cocktail made with limes, sugar, and sugarcane rum

caixa
a small drum with strings in the bottom that creates a sound like a snare drum

caju
cashew fruit

calculável
calculating

calor
hot

caminhão
truck

Canadá
Canada

canadense
Canadian

canção
song

caneta
pen

canil
kennel

cansado, cansada
tired

cantar
to sing

canto
I sing (present)

cantor, cantora
singer

cão
dog

caos
chaos

capaz
able

capital
capital

capitanias
territories awarded to Portuguese officials in the sixteenth century

capitão
captain

capítulo
chapter

capoeira
martial art that incorporates African dance

cardíaco
cardiac

careca
bald

carinho
affection

Carnaval
the equivalent of Mardi Gras, a week of festivities before Lent

carne de boi
beef

carne de porco
pork

carne seca
Brazilian beef jerky

caro, cara
expensive, dear (informal)

carro
car

cartão de crédito
postcard

cartão postal
postcard

cartão telefônico
phone card

cartaz
poster

cartões
cards

casa
house

casa de câmbio
currency exchange agency

casaco
coat

casado, casada
married

casal
couple

casar-se
to get married

castanho
brown, chestnut color

catálogo telefônico
phone book

catar (inf.)
to look for (colloquial)

catedral
cathedral

catorze
fourteen

cavaquinho
a small, four-string, guitar-like instrument created in

Portugal that later inspired the ukulele

cebola
onion

cedo
early

cego, cega
blind

cem
one hundred

censor
censor

cento e um, cento e uma
one hundred and one

central
central

centro
center

centro estudantil
student center

centro-oeste
central-west

certo
correct

cerveja
beer

céu
sky

chá
tea

chamada a cobrar
collect call

chamar
to call

chamar de
to call (someone or something a name)

chamar-se
to call oneself

chato, chata
boring

chave
key

checo, checa
Czech

chegar
to arrive

cheques de viagem
traveler's checks

Chile
Chile

chileno, chilena
Chilean

China
China

chinês, chinesa
Chinese

chocolate
chocolate

chover
to rain

chucalho
a shaker instrument made by putting metal cans together and filling them with rocks, sand, or beans

churrasco
Brazilian barbecue

ciclista
cyclist

ciclo
cycle, ring

cidade
city

cinco
five

cinema
movies, cinema

cinema novo
Brazilian cinematic movement

cinqüenta
fifty

cinto
belt

ciúme
jealousy

claramente
clearly

claridade
clarity

clarinete
clarinet

clima
weather

clímax
climax

clínica
clinic

clube
club, gym

coberto
covered

cochilo
nap

código
code

código de área
area code

código internacional
country code

colocar
to put, to place

Colombia
Colombia

colombiano, colombiana
Colombian

com
with

com licença
excuse me, sorry

começar
to start

comédia
comedy

comediante
comedian

comemorado, comemorada
celebrated

comer
to eat

comercial
commercial

comida
food

companheiro, companheira
friends, partners

competir
to compete

completar
to complete

complexo
complex

complô
scheme

compor
to compose

compositor
composer

comprar
to buy

compreender
*to understand,
to comprehend*

compreensível
comprehensible

computador
computer

comunicação
communication

comunicar
to communicate

concerto
concert

concorrentes
competitors

condutor
conductor

conferência
conference

confortável
comfortable

conhecer
to know (people, places)

conseguir
*to achieve,
to get*

conspirador
conspirer

constipado
*congested
(by a cold)*

construir
to construct

consulado
consulate

**consultor,
consultora**
consultant

**consumido,
consumida**
consumed

consumidor
consumer, client

conta
bill, account

**contador,
contadora**
accountant

contagem
act of counting

contente
happy

contra
against

conversa
conversation, talk (n.)

conversível
*convertible,
capable of
being converted*

convosco
*with you (pl.)
(archaic)*

Copacabana
*famous Brazilian
beach located in
Rio de Janeiro*

cor
color

coração
heart

cordial
cordial

corrente, colar
necklace

correr
to run

corrigir
to correct

Costa Rica
Costa Rica

costa-riquenho
Costa Rican

**costureiro,
costureira**
*clothes
designer,
dressmaker*

convencer-se de
*to convince
oneself of*

crachá
*identification
tag*

crédito
credit

criança
child

criatura
creature

crime
crime

cru, crua
raw

cruel
cruel

Cuba
Cuba

cuíca
*drum-like instrument with a
stiff string upon
which the player
slides his fingers
up and down
to produce a
squeaky sound*

cuidado
*care, (be) careful
(exclamation)*

cultura
culture

cultural
cultural

cunhada
sister-in-law

cunhado
brother-in-law

curável
curable

curioso
curious

curtir
to enjoy (slang)

Curupira
*human-like
creature whose*

feet are backwards; brings bad luck or death to those who see him

cyber café
Internet café

D. Pedro I
Dom Pedro I, the Emperor of Brazil

D. Pedro II
Dom Pedro II, son of D. Pedro I and Emperor of Brazil

dado
dice

dançar
to dance

dar
to give

dar sinal
to have a dial tone

dar uma volta
to go on a short trip

de repente
suddenly, all of sudden

debaixo de
under

decidir-se a
to decide to

décimo, décimo
tenth

décimo-primeiro, décima-primeira
eleventh

décimo-segundo, décima-segunda
twelfth

dedicar-se a
to dedicate oneself to

defronte de
facing, in front of

deitar-se
to go to bed, to retire

deixar
to leave

deixar um recado
to leave a message

dela
her

dele
his

deles, delas
theirs

delito
crime

demais
too much

dente de alho
garlic cloves

dentista
dentist

dentro de
inside

depois de amanhã
day after tomorrow

descansado, descansada
rested

descansar
to rest

desculpe, desculpa
sorry

desde
since

desejar
to wish, to desire

desenvolvimento
development

desligar o telefone
to hang up the phone

destruidor
destroyer

detector
detector

detrás de
behind

deus
god

devagar
slowly

dever de casa
homework

dez
ten

dezembro
December

dezenove
nineteen

dezesseis
sixteen

dezessete
seventeen

dezoito
eighteen

dia
day

Dia da Independência
Independence Day

Dia de Natal
Christmas Day

Dia de São Patrício
Saint Patrick's Day

Dia dos Namorados
Valentine's Day

dicionário
dictionary

difícil
difficult

digestível
digestable

dinastia
dynasty

dinheiro
money

diretor, diretora
director

dito
said

divertir-se
to entertain oneself, to have fun

dividido
divided

divorciado, divorciada
divorced

dizer
to say

dó
pity

doce
sweet

documento
document

doente
sick

dois, duas
two

dólares
dollars

domingo
Sunday

dominó
domino

Dona
a title of respect for women, as in Dona Maria

dor
pain

dormindo
asleep

dormir
to sleep

doze
twelve

droga
drug, drugs

drogaria
drugstore

durável
durable

duzentos, duzentas
two hundred

e
and

econômica
economic

Ecuador
Ecuador

editor
editor

educacional
educational

egípcio, egípcia
Egyptian

Egito
Egypt

ela
she, her

ele
he, him

eles, elas
they, them

elefante
elephant

elegância
elegance

elegante
elegant

eletrônico, eletrônica
electronic

em
in

em cima de
on top

em frente de
in front of

embaixada
embassy

embaixo de
under

emocional
emotional

empregado, empregada
employee, maid

encantado, encantada
a pleasure, nice to meet you

encontrar
to find

encontrar-se
to find oneself

endereço
address

engenheiro, engenheira
engineer

engraçado, engraçada
funny

enjoado, enjoada
sick, bored, boring

enquanto
while

ensaio
essay, rehearsal

então
then

entender
to understand

entrar em
to enter

entregue
handed, given

envelope
envelope

envergonhado, envergonhada
embarassed

equatoriano, equatoriana
Ecuadorian

erro
error, mistake

escadas
stairs

escola
school

escola primária
elementary school

escolher
to choose

escrever
to write

escrito
written

escritório
office

escutar
to hear, to listen

especialista
specialist

espelho
mirror

esporte
sport

esposo, esposa
spouse

esquecer-se de
to forget to

esquema
scheme, plan

esquina
corner

esse, essa
this

essencial
essential

esses, essas
these

estado
state

estar
to be

estatura
mediana
average height

este, esta
this

estudante
student

estudar
to study

estudioso,
estudiosa
studious

estupefato,
estupefata
stunned

eu
I

Europa
Europe

evitável
avoidable

exame
exam

excelente
excellent

excepcional
exceptional

excitado,
excitada
aroused

excluir
to exclude

exigir
to demand

exótico
exotic

explicações
explanations

explicar
to explain

explicável
explainable

faca
knife

façanha
feat

fácil
easy

Fado
*Portuguese
musical style*

fala
*speech,
language*

falar
to speak

falsificável
falsifiable

família
family

familiar
*familiar, per-
taining to family*

famoso, famosa
famous

farmacêutico,
farmacêutica
pharmacist

farmácia
drugstore

fatal
fatal

favor
favor

fazer
to do, to make

fazer a barba
to shave

fazer as pazes
to make peace

fazer compras
to buy

fazer de conta
to pretend

fazer exercícios
to exercise

fazer falta
to miss, to lack

fazer greve
to go on strike

fazer um
telefonema
*to make a
phone call*

federal
federal

feijão
beans

feijoada
*Brazilian black
bean and
pork stew*

feio, feia
ugly

feira
street market

feito
made, done

felicidade
happiness

feliz
happy

Feliz Natal
Merry Christmas

felizmente
fortunately

fenomenal
phenomenal

ferias
vacation

fervor
fervor

festa
party

festa de despedida
going-away party

fevereiro
February

ficar
to be (situated), to become, to stay

filha
daughter

filho
son

Filipinas
Philippines

filme
movie

fim de semana
weekend

físico (adj.)
physical

físico (n.)
physicist

fluentemente
fluently

fora
outside

forte
strong, stocky

fósforo
match

fóssil
fossil

fotógrafo, fotógrafa
photographer

fraco, fraca
weak

França
France

francês, francesa
French

frase
phrase

freguês, freguesa
customer

freqüência
frequency

frio
cold

frios
cold cuts

fuga
escape

fundamental
fundamental

futebol
soccer

futebol de salão
indoor soccer

futuro
future, future tense

fuzil
rifle

gancho
handset

ganho
won

garagem
garage

garçom
waiter

garçonete
waitress

garfo
fork

gasto
spent

gato
cat

genro
son-in-law

gente
people

gerente
manager

gesto
gesture

ginásio
gym

gordo, gorda
fat

gostar de
to like

gota
drop

Grã-bretanha
Great Britain

gramática
grammar

grande
big

Grécia
Greece

grego, grega
Greek

grúa
forklift

Guanabara
beach/locality in Rio de Janeiro

guaraná
a tropical berry found in the Amazon, the main ingredient in a Brazilian soft drink

guarda
policeman

guardanapo
napkin

guerra
war

guia
guide

guitarra
electric guitar

guri
young boy, indigenous origin word

Haiti
Haiti

haitiano, haitiana
Haitian

haver
to exist, to have

hebreu, hebréia
Hebrew

hindu
Hindu

hoje
today

Holanda
Holland

holandês, holandesa
Dutch

hora, horas
hour, hours

horrível
horrible

hospital
hospital

hotel
hotel

húmido, húmida
humid

humor
humor

ideal
ideal

idealismo
idealism

idéia
idea

idêntico, idêntica
identical

identidade
identity

idoso, idosa
elderly

igreja
church

igualmente
likewise, same here

ilegal
illegal

imagem
image

imediatamente
immediately

impedir
to impede

impor
to impose

importância
importance

importante
important

impossível
impossible

imprescindível
essential

impressionado, impressionada
impressed

incluído, incluída
included

incluir
to include

incomparável
incomparable

India
India

indiano, indiana
Indian

inevitável
inevitable

inferior
inferior

infinitivo pessoal
personal infinitive

informação
information

informar
to inform

Inglaterra
England

inglês, inglesa
English

insistência
insistence

inspetor
inspector

instrutor
instructor

inteligente
intelligent

internacional
international

interurbano
long distance

inventar
invent, to

inventor
inventor

inverno
winter

investir
to invest

Ipanema
famous beach in Rio de Janeiro

ir
to go

Irã
Iran

iraniano, iraniana
Iranian

Iraque
Iraq

iraquiano, iraquiana
Iraqi

Irlanda
Ireland

irlandês, irlandesa
Irish

irmã
sister

irmão
brother

irritado, irritada
irritated

Israel
Israel

israelense
Israeli

isso
this (neutral, abstract)

Itália
Italy

italiano, italiana
Italian

já
already

Jacarepaguá
locality in São Paulo

Jamaica
Jamaica

jamaicano, jamaicana
Jamaican

jamais
ever, never

janeiro
January

janela
window

jantar
*to have dinner,
dinner (n.)*

Japão
Japan

**japonês,
japonesa**
Japanese

jeito
way

**joelho de porco
defumado**
*smoked ham
hocks*

jogar
*to play (a sport
or a game)*

jornal
newspaper

jornaleiro
*newspaper
seller*

jornalista
*reporter,
journalist*

jovem (adj.)
young

jovem (n.)
youngster

juiz, juíza
judge

julho
July

junho
June

juntos, juntas
together

lá
there, over there

lambada
*African-inspired
dance and
musical style*

lamentável
lamentable

lápis
pencil

laranja
orange

lava a seco
dry-cleaners

lavar
to wash

lavar-se
to wash oneself

legume
*legume,
vegetable*

leite
milk

lembrança
*remembrance,
souvenir*

lembrar-se
to remember to

ler
to read

lhe
*to you, him,
her (indirect
pronoun)*

liberdade
liberty

lição
lesson

licor
liqueur

ligação direta
direct call

ligar
to call

limpo, limpa
clean

lindo, linda
beautiful

lingüiça
*Brazilian chorizo
or pepperoni*

Lisboa
Lisbon

livraria
bookstore

livro
book

lixo
trash

local
local

loção
lotion

loja
store

loja de roupa
clothing store

loja de sapatos
shoestore

longe de
far from

louco, louca
crazy

louro, loura
blond

lugar
place

maçã
apple

machucar-se
to hurt oneself

Madeira
*island in the
Atlantic Ocean
belonging
to Portugal*

madrasta
stepmother

madrinha
godmother

mãe
mother

magro, magra
thin

maio
May

mais
more

mais ou menos
so-so

mamãe
mom, mommy

Manaus
*city in the north
of Brazil, capital
of the state of
Amazonas*

mapa
map

mar
sea, ocean

maravilha
wonder

maravilhoso,
maravilhosa
wonderful

março
March

marido
husband

marrom
brown

mecânico
mechanic

medicina
medicine

médico
doctor

meia-noite
midnight

meio-dia
noon, midday

melão
melon

melhor
better, best

menina
girl

menino
boy

menos
minus

menos
less

mentir
to lie

mentor
mentor

mesa
table

mesmo
same

meu, minha
(plural: meus,
minhas)
my

mexicano,
mexicana
Mexican

México
Mexico

mil
one thousand

milionário
millionaire

Minas Gerais
*a state in the
southeast
of Brazil*

miserável
miserable

Moçambique
Mozambique

mochila
backpack

moderno,
moderna
modern

moleque
*young boy,
pejorative*

momento
moment

morar
to live (reside)

moreno,
morena
dark-skinned

morto
died

morto, morta
dead

mosca
fly (insect)

motor
motor, engine

MPB, Música
Popular
Brasileira
*Brazilian Popu-
lar Music*

mucama
*young slave girl
who fetches
things*

muito
a lot, very

muito prazer
nice to meet you

mulher
wife, spouse

múltipla escolha
multiple choice

museu
museum

música
music, song

música
sertaneja
*Brazilian coun-
try music*

músico, música
musician

na semana
passada
last week

nacional
national

nada
nothing

namorada
girlfriend

namorado
boyfriend

não
no

natural
natural

natureza
nature

nau, navio
boat, ship

neblina
fog

negociável
negotiable

nem . . . nem
neither . . . nor

nenhum,
nenhuma
not one

nervoso,
nervosa
nervous

neta
granddaughter

neto
grandson

nevar
to snow

neve
snow

Nheengatu
indigenous language of Brazil

Nicarágua
Nicaragua

nicaragüense
Nicaraguan

ninguém
nobody

noiva
fiancée, bride

noivo
fiancé, groom

nome
name

nono, nona
ninth

nora
daughter-in-law

Nordeste
northeast

normal
normal

norte
north

nós
we

Nossa!
Wow!

nosso, nossa
our

nove
nine

novecentos, novecentas
nine hundred

novembro
November

noventa
ninety

novo, nova
new

nu, nua
naked

nublado
cloudy

número
number

número de telefone
phone number

nunca
never

o, os
the (masc.)

obrigado, obrigada
thank you

óbvio
obvious

óculos
eyeglasses

ocupado, ocupada
busy

oficial
official

oi
hi

oitavo, oitava
eighth

oitenta
eighty

oito
eight

oitocentos, oitocentas
eight hundred

olá
hi

óleo
vegetable oil

olhar para
to look at

olhar-se
to look at oneself

onde
where

ontem
yesterday

onze
eleven

opa!
hey!

operário, operária
factory worker

opositor
opposing

orelha de porco
pig's ear

orelhão
telephone booth

órfão
orphan

organizável
organizable

órgão
organ

original
original

ostensível
ostensible

ótima
great

outono
autumn, fall

outro, outra
other

outubro
October

ouvir
to hear, to listen

ovo
egg

paciência
patience

padaria
bakery

padrasto
stepfather

padrinho
godfather

pagar
to pay

página
page

pago
paid

pagode
type of backyard samba typical of Rio

pai
father

pálido, pálida
pale

Panamá
Panama

panamenho, panamenha
Panamanian

pandeiro
large tambourine that is played fast and sometimes spun on one finger for show

pão
bread

papai
dad, daddy

papel
paper

papelaria
stationary store

para
to

parcial
partial

parecer-se com
to look like

parque
park

partir
to leave

passado, passada
past

passar
to pass, to overcome, to approve

pássaro
bird

passável
passable

pastor
pastor

pato
duck

pau
wood

pé de porco
pig's foot

pediatra
pediatrician

pedir
to ask for

pegar
to catch

pente
comb

pentear-se
to brush/comb oneself

perdã
pardon, sorry

perder
to lose

perfume
perfume

pergunta
question

permitir
to allow

Pernambuco
state in northeast Brazil

persistente
persistent

perto
close, nearby

peru
turkey

pêssego
peach

pessoa famosa
celebrity

pianista
pianist

piloto
pilot

pimenta do reino
black pepper

pimenta malagueta
hot pepper sauce

pincel
paintbrush

pior
worse, the worst

piranha
piranha

planeta
planet

plano
plane, leveled

pobre
poor

poder
to be able to, can, may

pois é
right, indeed

Pois não!
Sure!

Pois não?
May I help you?

polícia
police

polonês, polonesa
Polish

Polônia
Poland

popular
popular

populoso, populosa
populated

pôr
to put, to place

por favor
please

por gentileza
please (formal)

pôr na cadeia
put in jail

por obséquio
please (formal)

por quê
why

porém
but, however

porque
because

porta
door

Portugal
Portugal

possível
possible

posto
put, set

potência
power

potente
potent

poucos, poucas
few

prato
dish

prazer
pleasure

precisar de
to need

prédio
building

prender
to arrest

**preocupado,
preocupada**
worried

**preocupar-
se com**
to worry about

presentável
presentable

presente
gift

**presente
contínuo**
progressive
present

presidente
president

presunto
ham

pretérito
preterite tense

**prezado,
prezada**
dear (formal)

prima
cousin (female)

primavera
spring

**primeiro,
primeira**
first

primo
cousin (male)

proa
bow, front part
of the ship

problema
problem

**professor,
professora**
teacher,
professor

profissão
profession

programa
program

proposta
proposal

protetor
protector

prova
test

punha
he/she would
put (imperfect
tense)

quadro
board

qual
what, which

qualquer
any

quando
when

quanto, quanta
how much

**quantos,
quantas**
how many

quarenta
forty

quarta-feira
Wednesday

quarto, quarta
fourth

quatro
four

**quatrocentos,
quatrocentas**
four hundred

que
then, that, what

queijo
cheese

queixar-se de
to complain
about

quem
who

querer
to want

**querido,
querida**
dear (informal)

quilombo
village of ma-
rooned slaves

**quinhentos,
quinhentas**
five hundred

quinta-feira
Thursday

quinto, quinta
fifth

quinze
fifteen

rabo de porco
pig's tail

racional
rational

rádio
radio

raiz
root

ranking
ranking

rapaz
young man

rápido, rápida
fast

reagir
to react

real, reais
Brazilian
currency

recado
message

receber
to receive

Recife
a city in north-
east Brazil

**reconhecido,
reconhecida**
recognized

recordar
to remember

refletir
to reflect, to think

refletor
reflector, reflecting

rei
king

relâmpago
lightening

remédios
medicines, medication

repenique
a medium-size drum, larger than a snare drum, played with a stick and one hand

réptil
reptile

República Checa
Czech Republic

respeitável
respectable

responder
to answer

ressaca
hangover

restaurante
restaurant

reunir-se
to get together

revistas
magazines

rico, rica
rich

rio
river

Rio Capibaribe
Capibaribe River, a river in the state of Pernambuco

Rio Grande do Sul
a state in the south of Brazil

rir
to laugh

rir-se de
to laugh at

roxo
purple

rua
street

ruim
bad

ruivo, ruiva
redhead, redheaded

rumor
rumor

sábado
Saturday

saber
to know (information, skills)

sair
to go out, leave

sal
salt

sala de aula
classroom

salão de beleza
beauty salon

samba
a distinctly Brazilian musical style heavily influenced by the African drumming tradition

samba canção
also called the samba song, a slower samba piece with romantic lyrics put to music

samba enredo
fast, highly rhythmic samba with words and lyrics sung during Carnaval

Sambódromo
the place where samba schools parade every year in Rio de Janeiro

sanduíche
sandwich

Santa Catarina
a state in the south of Brazil

santo
saint

sapataria
shoe store

sapo
frog

satisfeito, satisfeita
satisfied

saudações cordiais
cordially

seção
section

secretária
secretary

secretária (eletrônica)
answering machine (literally "the electronic secretary")

sedutor
seductor

segunda-feira
Monday

segundo, segunda
second

seis
six

seiscentos, seiscentas
six hundred

semana
week

sempre
always

senha
code

senhor
mister

senhora
ma'am, lady

sensacional
sensational

sentar-se
to sit

sentar-se
to sit oneself

senzala
slave quarters

separado, separada
separated

ser
to be

sério, séria
serious

servir
to serve

sessenta
sixty

sete
seven

setecentos, setecentas
seven hundred

setembro
September

setenta
seventy

sétimo, sétima
seventh

Seu
abbreviation for senhor, a title of respect

seu, sua (plural: seus, suas)
your

sexta-feira
Friday

sexto, sexta
sixth

shopping
mall

si
himself/herself

sim
yes

simpático
nice

simples
simple

sinal
dial tone

sinistro
sinister

sinto muito
I am terribly sorry

situação
situation

sobre
over, on top

sobrinha
niece

sobrinho
nephew

sóbrio, sóbria
sober

socialista
socialist

sócio, social
business partner

socorro
help

sofá
sofa

sogra
mother-in-law

sogro
father-in-law

sol
sun, sunny

solteiro, solteira
single

sonho
dream

sopa
soup

subir
to go up

sucuri
anaconda

sudeste
southeast

Suécia
Sweden

sueco, sueca
Swedish

Suíça
Switzerland

suíço, suíça
Swiss

sul
south

superior
superior

supermercado
supermarket

surdo
a large drum with a low but loud sound ("surdo" means deaf in Portuguese)

surpreendente
surprising

surpreender-se com
to be surprised

tá
short for está

tailandês, tailandesa
Thai

Tailândia
Thailand

tal
such

talento
talent

tamanho
size

também
also

também não
(not) either, neither

tamborim
a small, short drum played very fast with a stick

tanga
short bikini or loincloth

tanto, tanta
so much

tanto . . . quanto
as much. . .as

tantos, tantas
so many

tão . . . quanto
as . . . as

tarde
late

tarefa
task, homework

tatu
armadillo

táxi
taxi

tchau
bye

telefone
telephone

telefone sem fio
cordless phone

telefonema
telephone call

telefonista, ajuda ao assinante
operator, directory assistance

televisão
television

tempo
time, climate

tempo
weather

tenista
tennis player

tenor
tenor

ter
to have

ter medo
to be afraid

terça-feira
Tuesday

terceiro, terceira
third

terminar
to finish

terra
earth, land

Tetra
fourth soccer championship

teu, tua (plural: teus, tuas)
your

tia
aunt

Tijuca
locality in Rio de Janeiro

til
tilde

tio
uncle

tipo
type

tirar
to take

título
title

tocar
to play (an instrument), to touch

todo, toda
all, entire

todos, todas
all

tomar
to drink

tomar café
to have breakfast, to drink coffee

tórax
thorax

trabalhar
to work

trabalho
work, paper

tradicional
traditional

tranqüilo, tranqüila
calm

transferência
transfer

transferir
to transfer

trânsito
traffic

trazer
to bring

trem
train

trema
dieresis

três
three

treze
thirteen

trezentos, trezentas
three hundred

trinta
thirty

triste
sad

Tropicália
psychedelic musical style created by Caetano Veloso and others in the seventies

trovoada
thunder

tu
you

Tukano
indigenous language of Brazil

Tupã
supreme being of the Tupi people

Tupi Guarani
indigenous language of Brazil

um milhão
one million

um, uma
one

usual
usual, or an extension of use

valor
value, valor

velho, velha
old

vendedor, vendedora
salesperson

vendedor, vendedora ambulante
street vendor

vender
to sell

Venezuela
Venezuela

venezuelano, venezuelana
Venezuelan

ventar
to be windy

ver
to see

verão
summer

verdade
truth

verduras
vegetables

vermelho, vermelha
red

vestir-se
to put on clothes, to dress oneself

vezes
times

viagem
trip

viajar
to travel

vigésimo, vigésima
twentieth

vinagre
vinegar

vindo
come, arrived

vinho
wine

vinte
twenty

vinte e dois, vinte e duas
twenty-two

vinte e três
twenty-three

vinte e um, vinte e uma
twenty-one

vir
to come, to arrive

virgem
virgin

visitar
to visit

visto
seen

viu
he/she saw (preterite)

viúvo
widower

viúva
widow

viver
to live

vizinho, vizinha
neighbor

você, vocês
you

voltar
to come back

voluntário
voluntary, volunteer

vontade
will

vós
you (pl.) (archaic)

vosso
yours (archaic)

vovó
grandma, granny

vovô
grandpa

xadrez
chess

xícara
cup

Yara
Tupi divinity

zinco
zinc

zulu
Zulu

INDEX